THE STORY OF THE CHURCH

The Story of the Church

by

A. M. RENWICK, M.A., D.D., D.LITT.

Professor of Church History,
The Free Church College, Edinburgh

WM. B.. EERDMANS PUBLISHING CO.
Grand Rapids, Michigan

First Edition: March 1958
Tenth printing, April 1978

Library of Congress Catalog
Card No. 59-6955

ISBN 0-8028-1163-9

PHOTOLITHOPRINTED BY EERDMANS PRINTING COMPANY
GRAND RAPIDS, MICHIGAN, UNITED STATES OF AMERICA

CONTENTS

PROLOGUE

FOR nearly two thousand years the Christian Church has exercised a profound influence upon the western world. Since the beginning of the nineteenth century its moral and spiritual influence has spread, in a greater or less degree, to almost all parts of the globe. No one, therefore, ought to be indifferent to the story of the Church of Christ.

Dr. H. M. Gwatkin defines church history as 'the spiritual side of the history of civilized peoples ever since our Master's coming'.[1] In other words, church history is the story of the Christian community and its relationship to the rest of the world throughout the ages. This study is not merely one which satisfies our curiosity as to what happened in past times; it is of great practical value for the present. Man is essentially the same in every age, although his surroundings and the circumstances of his life may differ. He has had, essentially, the same weaknesses and the same aspirations all through history. In spite of changing circumstances, and the presence or absence of certain factors, man has basically varied but little within historic times.

As we survey, then, the influences which at times led the Church to scale great heights of spiritual achievement, and consider also those elements which, in other periods, led her out into the dark and arid wilderness of error and moral decay, we are simply beholding what can be repeated in any epoch, in-

[1] H. M. Gwatkin, *Early Church History to* A.D. *313*, p. 4.

7

cluding our own, provided the contributing factors are present. To help guide our steps aright in the present we must know something of the past; and if the Church of God is to escape today the nemesis which always follows on certain lines of action, she must learn to ponder carefully the experiences of other days, whether these were good or evil. If it is true that secular history is 'philosophy teaching by examples', then church history is certainly the Christian religion teaching by examples.

As we look back upon the path by which the human race has arrived at its present position, we can scarcely avoid asking ourselves, 'Have the great events of history happened by chance, or can we trace behind these events the hand of Providence guiding all that comes to pass?' Even in secular history there is much which suggests a divine Providence directing the affairs of the world, age by age, and out of evil bringing good. Much more do we find this in church history. Consider, for example, how the Reformation was saved, just when it seemed that nothing could prevent Luther and his associates from being crushed. The emperor Charles V, having made a peace treaty with his enemy, the King of France, was trying to stamp out the new movement when there came a new distraction. The Mahometan Turks came marching up the Danube in their thousands, and were thundering at the gates of Vienna in the very heart of Europe. Thus Charles V had to make peace with his Protestant subjects and seek their help against the common enemy. As a result the Reformed Church escaped probable annihilation.

The history of the Church is simply an account of its success and its failure in carrying out Christ's great commission to 'go into all the world, and preach the gospel to every creature' and 'teach all nations'.[1] It may be divided as follows:

[1] Mk. xvi. 15; Mt. xxviii. 19, 20.

1. *Missionary activity*

This is the great story of the spiritual conquest of many lands, showing how the brave little band of disciples which went forth at Christ's call to preach the gospel originated forces which progressively influenced nation after nation, in spite of tremendous opposition throughout the centuries.

2. *Church organization*

Here we see the fulfilment of our Lord's words that, although His kingdom was like a grain of mustard seed, it would yet become a great tree sheltering the birds of the air (Lk. xiii. 19). The small and apparently weak Church became a mighty organization known throughout the earth. Its history shows its moral grandeur; it shows, too, certain defects arising from human weakness and the love of worldly pomp and power contrary to the spirit of the Master. We see many struggles between conflicting systems of church government, causing strife and division.

3. *Doctrine*

A part of church history is concerned with the development of doctrinal systems, for questions arose early as to what was the content of the gospel message. Hence attention must be given to Councils, heresies, excommunications, party divisions and similar developments, even when these are not very edifying. At the same time, there is revealed the uplifting spectacle of men and women who loved the truth and were ready to die for it.

4. *The effect on human life*

The gospel is shown to be as 'leaven hid in three measures of meal' (Mt. xiii. 33). The lives of innumerable individuals and of many nations have been transformed by the mighty power of the cross. Christian education and philanthropic agencies have exemplified the love of Christ to men, raising whole peoples to a new moral plane. It is a thrilling narrative, but there is the reverse side. Multitudes have been unfaithful to the great teachings of Christianity and have fallen back into worldliness and unbelief. Yet, as we shall see, the comforting fact emerges that God never 'left himself without witness' and that there have always been some devoted men and women 'whose hearts God had touched'.

CHAPTER I

THE APOSTOLIC AGE

'IN THE FULNESS OF TIME'

THE historical situation in the Empire when the gospel first began to be carried outside Palestine certainly suggests that a supreme Mind had been preparing the field, and that now all was ready for proclaiming to many nations the good tidings of salvation through the cross of Christ. A number of factors which greatly favoured the spread of the gospel may be noted.

1. The political unity of the Empire and the long peace had fostered commerce, which in turn sent business men all over the Roman world, many of whom carried the gospel along the trade routes on the excellent roads which had been built.

2. The conquests of Alexander between 334 and 326 B.C. spread the Greek language far and wide, thus providing the best medium ever known for expressing theological and philosophical ideas. The translation of the Old Testament into Greek in Alexandria about 200 B.C. predisposed many pagans in favour of monotheism.

3. In the cosmopolitan atmosphere of the Empire, where so many races and religions mingled together, men were losing faith in the pagan cults.

4. The moral condition of the world was deplorable. What it was like is revealed in the first chapter of the Epistle to the Romans as well as in the works of heathen writers. Slavery had produced shocking de-

11

terioration not only in the enslaved but also in the homes of their masters.

5. The fatalism and despair characteristic of the East were moving westward and affecting the outlook of the Roman world.

In these depressing conditions many were looking for a guiding star amid the gloom. They could not find it in the prevailing philosophies of Stoicism and Epicureanism. But at that moment, when every human system had been proved insufficient to save the soul, the Star of Bethlehem appeared, bringing hope to the world.

EARLY DAYS

Students who wish to understand the beginnings of church history must study the life of our Lord, and the life of Paul. Many books are available, but the best of all is the New Testament. We can also discover a certain amount from sub-apostolic Christian writers, and can glean something from secular authors such as Tacitus, Suetonius, Pliny and Josephus.

We may notice first the change which came over the apostles at the Day of Pentecost. As promised by Christ, they were 'endued with power from on high',[1] and then went forth to their colossal task in the strength of God. Disciples who before were very timid now became absolutely fearless.[2] Almost immediately afterwards the number of men converted in Jerusalem alone numbered 5,000, exclusive of women and children.[3]

Beginning at Jerusalem, the Christian faith soon spread far and wide. In Roman times communications by sea as well as by land were relatively easy, a factor which greatly helped the missionaries of the cross. Jews outside Palestine, who spoke Greek and were influenced by Greek culture, began to receive the gospel. Barnabas, a friend of Paul, a native of Cyprus, is

[1] See Acts ii.   [2] Acts iii, iv.   [3] Acts iv. 4.

typical of this very important class. Soon the good news was being carried to Samaria, and to Caesarea, on the Mediterranean Sea, and was being proclaimed freely to the Gentiles—a veritable revolution.[1] Then it went to Phoenicia, to Cyprus, and to the great city of Antioch in Syria.

The conversion of St. Paul (about 35 A.D.) was of surpassing importance to the Church, for he became the outstanding 'apostle to the Gentiles'. At Antioch, known as 'the Queen of the East', he and Barnabas did a most fruitful work among Jews and Gentiles. As this was a very important commercial centre, the gospel spread from here into wide areas both east and west. Among the Jewish groups encountered in every city, Paul and the other apostles found starting-points for their work of Empire-wide evangelization, even although the majority of the Jews rejected the gospel.

The conversion of so many Gentiles soon raised serious problems as to how far these new converts ought to be bound by the laws and ceremonies of the Jewish Church. Those known as Judaizers wanted the Gentiles to be circumcised, i.e. to become Jews first; thereafter they might become Christians, but Christians with a strong Jewish tinge. Fortunately for the Christian Church, Paul set his face resolutely against these tendencies.[2] The whole problem was thrashed out at the Council of Jerusalem in 49 A.D. There Paul gained a signal victory.[3] In spite of this, however, the question vexed the Church for many a long day. The Judaizers continued to dog Paul's steps to the very end of his life.

Anyone who wishes to understand the spread of Christianity in the early days should trace each of Paul's journeys on a good map, following the account in the book of Acts. We see him in Antioch,

---

[1] Acts viii, x, xi.　　[2] See Gal. ii. 7–16, iii. 1–11.
[3] See Acts xv. 1–29.

Cyprus, Pamphylia, Central Asia Minor, Cilicia, and Syria. Then he pushes on to Troas and across to Europe.[1]

After long years of incessant missionary labours Paul was arrested at the Temple in Jerusalem and conveyed to Caesarea for his own security.[2] For two whole years he was unjustly kept in prison in Caesarea by the unscrupulous Felix. In 59 A.D. he was conveyed to Rome for trial, and for another two years was kept a prisoner although 'in his own hired house'.[3] He preached his message freely to all who came to him —even to the soldiers who took their turn in standing guard over him. It was not long before many, even 'in Caesar's household', believed in Christ. During this period, also, Paul wrote some of his profoundest Epistles. He seems to have been set free in 61 A.D. and to have visited once more the regions where he had evangelized so successfully in previous years. We find him again in prison in Rome when he wrote the second Epistle to Timothy prior to his execution about 64 A.D. during the persecution under Nero.

All we know of Peter forbids us to think he was less active than Paul. His eager, impulsive heart would keep him constantly engaged in his Master's business all his days. As Paul was the apostle of the Gentiles in a special sense, so Peter was pre-eminently the apostle of the Jews. This would lead him to the great cities of the Empire where vast numbers of his countrymen were to be found. The small amount of evidence we have points to Peter's having been at Rome towards the end of his life and to his having died there as a martyr, perhaps at the same time as Paul, or at least in the same year. We may note, however, that there is no foundation for the claim of the Roman Church that Peter was Bishop of Rome for twenty-five years—from

---

[1] Acts xvi—xviii.   [2] See Acts xxi. 27–40, xxiii—xxvii.
[3] See Acts xxvii, xxviii.

42 to 67 A.D. Had Peter been there before 61 A.D., Paul could not have failed to mention him in the Epistles he wrote from that city just prior to that date. The fact that Peter probably visited Rome as an apostle would not make him Bishop of Rome, much less Pope of Rome. Apostles were not settled in one place like diocesan bishops. Indeed, at that time, and for long afterwards, there were no such bishops. It is, therefore, incorrect to speak of Rome as the 'See of Peter', or of the pope as occupying 'the chair' of Peter.

Remarkably little reliable knowledge has come down to us about the personal history of the various apostles. Their work has endured, but in many cases their own personal history has perished. The same applies to the founding of some very great and important churches. Thus, we have only a vague tradition that Mark founded the Church at Alexandria. Reliable history has no knowledge as to who founded the world-famous churches at Rome and at Carthage. Men returning to their own lands, from Jerusalem, after the Day of Pentecost must have done much to spread the gospel, as did Christian business men somewhat later.[1]

THE APOSTOLIC MESSAGE

What was the message delivered by the Church in those days? It is briefly summed up by Paul in 1 Cor. xv. 1-11. They never forgot the fact of sin—that men were lost. The very name 'Jesus' reminded them of this, for it means 'Saviour'. The resurrection was to them the crowning evidence that Jesus was all He claimed to be—the Son of God who had all power given unto Him. In their preaching they appealed to the testimony of many eye-witnesses who had seen Christ after His resurrection. The evidence was overwhelming. They also appealed to the marvels wrought in His name by His followers, and pointed out the wonders of His saving grace as seen in themselves and

[1] Acts viii. 26-40.

many others. So successful were they in spreading their teaching that eighteen years after the resurrection of Christ His followers were accused of 'turning the world upside down'.[1]

Through this 'good news' which they preached the lives of men and women were transformed. As the whole narrative shows, the chains of vice were broken and sinners were cleansed and raised to a higher spiritual plane by the power of God. The broken-hearted were comforted, the weak were made strong, the selfish learned to love their fellow-men and sacrifice themselves for the cause of Christ. Superstitions were swept away, idolatry vanished.[2] Even the slave, hitherto treated as less than human, and who could be sold or killed at the pleasure of his owner, was now given a place in the Christian Church as a child of God, and sat down at the same Communion Table with his master. The effects of all this on first-century communities were more than any of us can realize.

EARLY PERSECUTIONS

Christ warned His disciples 'If they have persecuted me, they will also persecute you'. 'The servant is not greater than his lord.'[3] The earliest persecutions came not from the Romans but from the Jews. At first the civil authorities scarcely distinguished between Christians and Jews, and extended to the former the privilege which was enjoyed by the latter of being a protected religion under Roman law. Probably one of the worst Jewish persecutions was that which followed on the death of Stephen, the first Christian martyr,[4] but in the accounts of Paul's travels there are continual references to the bitter opposition of Judaism to the gospel.

The Roman authorities could not understand the

---

[1] Acts xvii. 6..   Eph. iv. 24–32.   [3] Jn. xv. 20; Mt. v. 12.
[4] Acts vii, viii[2] 1, xviii. 12–17, xxi. 31–40.

claim that Christ was supreme and that all, even kings and emperors, must submit to Him. The Christians refused to conform to many accepted customs. They would have nothing to do with idolatry, and condemned the public games where gladiators fought in mortal combat to make sport for the spectators, and where innocent prisoners were thrown to the lions for the entertainment of the vast multitudes. They refused public office, and certain public duties, such as the burning of incense to the gods, or the pouring of libations, because such things were associated with pagan rites. The result was that they were regarded as a morose and intolerable people. Matters came to a crisis when, in 64 A.D., the emperor Nero accused the Christians of setting fire to the city of Rome. The public feeling against them was such that they were universally reviled. Even a writer of the eminence of Tacitus, who disliked Nero intensely, writes of Christianity as a 'most mischievous superstition'. He accuses them of 'abominations', and declares that 'they were put to death as enemies of mankind'.

The cruelties perpetrated at Rome in the Neronic persecution were unspeakable, and a vast number of Christians perished. Some were wrapped in the skins of wild beasts so that they would be more savagely attacked by dogs. Some were crucified; others were placed in barrels of pitch, or smeared with pitch and set on fire, and these living torches were used by Nero to illuminate his gardens as he drove about, enjoying this dreadful spectacle.

THE DESTRUCTION OF JERUSALEM

Before the Neronic persecution of the Christians had died down, terrible events in Palestine compelled the Romans to enter upon a life and death struggle with the Jews. For these events the Christians had no responsibility. The struggle was precipitated by the Zealots, a Jewish Nationalist party which had resolved to deliver their land from the Romans, by violence and massacre if need be. After the year 60 A.D. the Zealots had become so powerful that no other Jewish group could counteract their fierce and desperate propaganda.

The people had good cause for their discontent, for Roman administration was now very corrupt, and this presented the Zealots with their opportunity. At this time the Christians in Palestine were in an exceedingly difficult position, for they were hated equally by the Romans and by the Jews.

The day of God's wrath, so often foretold, was about to break. The conflict began when, in May 66 A.D., the Zealots massacred the Roman garrison in Jerusalem. In spite of some early Jewish victories, Titus surrounded the city four years later. Remembering Christ's warning (Mt. xxiv. 15), the Christians fled to Pella beyond Jordan and were saved. The terrible siege of Jerusalem began at Easter, when the city was crowded with the pilgrims who had come to observe the Feast of the Passover, and went on till September. Never have men fought with more desperate heroism than did the Jews then. Hundreds of thousands were slain by the sword; many others died from famine and pestilence. At last the Romans got possession of the Temple and ransacked all its treasures, including the most sacred vessels of the divine service. Finally, even the Holy of Holies was set on fire, and six weeks later all Jerusalem was completely subjugated.[1]

It was the end of an epoch. The old order had fulfilled its day and perished. The fanaticism and violence of the Zealots had been the occasion of bringing this destruction upon the beautiful, but unrepentant city which had so often 'killed the prophets', and 'stoned those that were sent to it', and had crucified the Lord of glory. The removal of the Temple, with its priests, ritual, and ceremonial, was a further indica-

[1] Cf. Christ's prophecy, Lk. xix. 41–44; Mt. xxiv. 2; Mk. xiii. 2.

tion that old things had passed away and that a better day had dawned. Christ, by His death, had opened the way to God and brought in a more spiritual worship.

THE ORGANIZATION OF THE EARLY CHURCH
AND ITS SPECIAL GIFTS

A careful study reveals that in the apostolic age some officers in the Church were temporary and others permanent. To the first class belonged apostles, prophets, and in one sense evangelists; to the second, the office of elder (*presbuteros*) or bishop (*episcopos*); and that of the deacon (*diakonos*). To understand certain developments in church history we must know something about these offices.

The most outstanding of all was the *apostle*. The word means one who is 'sent', a messenger. In the wider sense, this applied to men like Barnabas and Epaphroditus.[1] The 'twelve apostles', however, were in a special class. The New Testament tells us of their qualifications. They were chosen directly by Christ and commissioned personally by Him to spread the gospel, organize the Church, and work miracles. They received special revelations and a special authority directly from the Lord and were empowered by God to communicate inspired teaching to the Church for all ages. Their utterances took rank as Scriptures inspired by the Holy Spirit.[2]

It is easily seen that the apostles were a unique class appointed by Christ to establish His Church in the world at a time when special guidance and special instruction were called for. Their supernatural gifts and authority were such that they left no successors. When the last apostle died he left behind him none other of the same class.

The New Testament *prophets* were inspired announcers of the truth, whether dealing with the

---

[1] Cf. Phil. ii. 25; Acts xiv. 4, 14 (Greek text).
[2] 1 Cor. ii. 13, vii. 40; 1 Thes. ii. 13.

present, the future, or the past. There were many of them in the early days of the Church, and they are classed as next to the apostles.[1] They gradually disappeared from the scene and are not met with after the third quarter of the second century. We can realize their immense importance to the Church in the days before the Canon of the New Testament was formed, and before there was a trained ministry.

From a scriptural point of view, the *evangelist* was temporary only in the sense that he preached the gospel to those outside the Church and planted churches where they did not previously exist. He differed from an apostle in not possessing of necessity any supernatural powers. He travelled about, and his duties were mainly the conversion of sinners and the building up of a congregation which he left afterwards to a settled ministry. Throughout the ages evangelists have done a great work in times of moral darkness and spiritual decline by acting as auxiliaries to the regular ministry. Philip and Timothy were typical evangelists.

When we turn to consider the permanent officers of the Church, we find that in the days of the apostles, elders and deacons were appointed and their duties defined.[2] The office of *elder* is variously described in the New Testament as bishop, pastor, teacher, preacher, minister, steward, angel (i.e. messenger). The various terms mentioned referred to the same officer but each presented a different aspect of their work. Thus 'pastor' indicated their duty to 'shepherd the flock' of Christ. 'Bishop', a word used to translate the Greek *episcopos,* indicated that they were 'overseers', and Paul shows us that as 'overseers' they had to 'feed the church of God'.[3] That the 'presbuteros' and 'episcopos' (elder and bishop) were the same is shown by many facts. Thus Paul addressed his letter

---

[1] 1 Cor. xii. 28; Eph. ii. 20.   [2] 1 Tim. iii. 1–13; 1 Pet. v. 1–4.
[3] Acts xx. 17–28.

to the Philippians to 'the bishops and deacons'. It was
a small church in a small city, yet it had a plurality of
bishops. It is not uncommon in the early Church to
find a large number of bishops in a small area. They
could not be bishops in our modern sense. Then,
again, the elders (*presbuteroi*) at Ephesus are expressly
called 'bishops of the flock' (*episcopoi*). Furthermore,
the qualifications of elders and bishops were the same.
Scarcely any scholar today would dispute the words of
the late Dr. J. B. Lightfoot, Bishop of Durham, and an
undoubted authority: 'It is a fact now generally
recognized by theologians of all shades of opinion,
that in the language of the New Testament, the same
officer in the Church is called indifferently bishop and
elder, or presbyter.'[1]

The term deacon comes from the Greek *diakonos*
meaning a *servant* or *minister*. In the English New
Testament whenever the reference is to those who were
administering the funds and property given for the
poor, the word is rendered *deacon*. In this sense it
refers to a definite class composed of men of high
Christian character.[2] The office was very well known in
the early Church, and it has been generally believed
in the past that the 'seven' set apart by the apostles
were the first members of this order.[3] This is now
doubted by certain scholars, but it is in accordance
with the view of Irenaeus in the second century. The
seven were appointed expressly to attend to the administration of charitable relief among the poor, so that
the apostles could be freed from 'the serving of tables'
and give themselves 'continually to prayer, and to the
ministry of the word'. This certainly expresses the
reasons why deacons were given a place in the Church,
whatever view we may take of the seven. They were
appointed as helpers in the administration and general
business of the Church, so that the other ranks of the

---

[1] *Commentary on Philippians*, p. 93.
[2] 1 Tim. iii. 12, 13; Phil. i. 1.   [3] Acts vi. 1–6.

ministry might dedicate themselves more fully to the higher spiritual exercises of their calling. In the course of history, the various bodies which make up the Christian Church have differed considerably in their teaching regarding the position and functions of the deacon.

While the apostles lived, their authority was decisive; but even in their day Councils were held, as in 49 A.D., at Jerusalem. Later, the Councils were of a regional character, but the churches in the various regions (although autonomous) kept up a correspondence with one another and maintained fraternal unity in the love of Christ. Later still, from 325 A.D. onwards, came the great Ecumenical Councils which tried to lay down laws for the Church Universal.

The worship of the early Church was modelled upon the simple service of the synagogue rather than upon the ritualistic service of the Temple, and the worshippers really came into vital touch with God. The result was a most powerful and effective Church. We are astonished at what they accomplished. With no worldly grandeur, with little social influence, without even church buildings, those early Christians went on from strength to strength, in spite of the opposition of the great Roman Empire and the bitter animosity of a sinful, pagan world which hated them because the purity of the Christians' lives condemned their own lack of moral standards.

The very essence of church organization and Christian life and worship in the first two centuries was simplicity. There was an absence of that formalism and pomp which took possession of the field in later times when spiritual life declined. Christians met for worship whenever they could, often in private homes and sometimes in more public places, such as 'the school of Tyrannus'. Their worship was free and spontaneous under the guidance of the Holy Spirit, and had not yet become inflexible in its form through the use of manuals of devotion. The Church was vigorously active. Not only the pastor but also many of those present took part in the services, for to them the priesthood of all believers was a tremendous reality.

By the end of the first century, the gospel had been carried far from its starting-point in Jerusalem. No amount of persecution could stop it. Towards the East it had reached Mesopotamia and Parthia. In the West it had spread to Gaul and Spain. The Church was growing already in the great cities of Rome, Alexandria, and Carthage. In Antioch and Ephesus as well as in Corinth, it was very strong. Christian groups were to be found scattered throughout Syria, Arabia and Illyria. Such was the record of seventy years' work in the face of constant opposition.

CHAPTER II

THE SECOND CENTURY

THE first seventy years of the second century constitute one of the obscurest periods in church history. The beginning of this period coincided with the death of the apostle John at Ephesus. He had returned from his exile in the lonely isle of Patmos when the persecution under Domitian ceased on the death of this emperor in 96 A.D. Through personal disappointments Domitian had become suspicious and embittered and had established a reign of terror throughout the Empire. Near the end of his life he turned fiercely on the Christians especially in the East. Later ages looked back upon him as almost a second Nero.

THE WRITINGS OF THE EARLY CHURCH

The passing away of the apostolic band made it more difficult for the Church to tread with confidence the path which led into an unknown future. Although Clement of Rome tells us that the apostles, knowing that difficulties would arise as to the oversight of the Church, had made provision for the appointment of ministers (bishops or presbyters, and deacons), we nevertheless become conscious of a great change in the quality of those who led the Church in this century. They were good men up to a point, and their writings compare favourably with those of the secular authors of the period; but they were obviously neither so spiritual nor so lucid as those who wrote the books of the sacred Canon. It may be helpful to refer to some of their more important works.

The Epistle of Clement of Rome is interesting as being probably the earliest of the sub-apostolic writings. It was written in 96 A.D. to the church at Corinth where there had been certain unpleasant divisions. Irenaeus, writing about a century later, says that Clement was the third Bishop of Rome. There is, however, no suggestion in Clement's Epistle that he had authority over any church other than his own. This is striking in view of the claims for supremacy always made by the Roman Catholic Church for the Bishop of Rome. In fact, Clement himself, like Paul and Luke (in the Acts of the Apostles), always uses the terms 'bishop' and 'presbyter' as being interchangeable. We cannot read Clement's lengthy letter without being deeply impressed by his earnestness, by the constant appeal to Scripture, both Old Testament and New, especially the Pauline Epistles, and by his deeply evangelical tone whenever he touches upon atonement for sin.

The next two sub-apostolic writers are chiefly interesting as showing the vagaries of churchmen who lay aside the divine Word given by apostles and prophets and follow their own imaginations. These are Barnabas, who wrote about 132 A.D., and Hermas who wrote *The Shepherd* between 140 and 150 A.D. Their imaginations ran riot. They both cherished strange and fanciful ideas, the former about Mosaic Law, and the latter about the forgiveness of sins through baptism.

The Teaching of the Lord through the Twelve Apostles to the Gentiles (the Didache) is regarded by some scholars as very early because of its primitive outlook. Others maintain that it was written somewhat later than the middle of the second century in some remote quarter of Syria or Palestine, and that this accounts for the primitive element. Early features remained largely unchanged in this backwater of the Church. It is very much coloured by Jewish views, is in parts legalistic and unspiritual, and lays great stress on fasts and ascetic practices such as abstaining from bodily desires. In this, especially, it goes quite beyond what is laid down in the New Testament. Baptism, it is interesting to note, may be performed by immersion or by pouring of water on the head three times. Both the minister and the candidate ought to fast previously. As in the case of *The Shepherd*, prophets have still a place in the Church but are losing influence, and rules are laid down for a very close scrutiny of their claims, to save the Church from imposture. The same tendency was noticeable everywhere, and by the end of the second century the work of prophets had virtually ceased.

Ignatius, Bishop of Antioch, who was martyred at Rome between 110 and 117 A.D., is one of the most remarkable and puzzling figures in church history. He wrote seven Epistles to various churches when on his way to Rome to be put to death. He dealt with the atonement and the incarnation (but more especially with the early heresy known as Docetism now threatening the Church), with the Judaizers, and with the subject of the Episcopate. Docetism taught that Christ during His life had only a phantasmal body and not a real one, and that His sufferings were therefore illusory. To meet the heretics Ignatius stressed the importance of unity and extolled obedience to the authority of the bishop as the best means of maintaining it. He wanted to have the *episcopos* in undisputed control, and because he did not see this in any church other than his own he emphasized the virtues of monarchical episcopacy as strongly as possible. To the Trallians he wrote: 'Respect the bishop as a type of God, and the presbyters as the council of God, and the college of the apostles. Apart from these there is not even the name of a Church.' This, like similar statements of his elsewhere, is almost blasphemous. He assigns a most important place to the presbytery as well as the bishop, and in this we may have a clue as to his real meaning.

We have already seen the sense in which the terms *presbyter* (or elder) and *bishop* were understood in early days and noted that these terms referred to the same person.[1] By the time of Ignatius, in Antioch and other places in the East, one of the presbyters had been chosen to preside over the others. He had become a permanent pastor and president of the other presbyters or elders, who helped and advised him in the work of the Church. This president is the man whom Ignatius calls *bishop* because he is *episcopos* or 'overseer'. He is still a presbyter, but has become a permanent pastor or overseer. This view is borne out by the fact that each of Ignatius' seven Epistles is addressed to the church concerned and not to a bishop. Even in writing to Rome, he makes no mention of any bishop there.

Polycarp of Smyrna is easily the greatest saint and martyr of the second century known to us. He was a disciple of John the Apostle, and since, when he was burnt at the stake in 156 A.D., he was some 86 years of age, he must have been about 30 years old when John died. Irenaeus, who was his pupil, related that Polycarp often referred to the apostles, especially to John. He was a man of simple and beautiful faith, and of a loving heart. In 155 A.D. he visited Rome to discuss the vexed question of the date of Easter. While there he met Bishop Anicetus of Rome on equal terms, and, although they failed to agree on the matter under discussion, they nevertheless remained excellent friends. Polycarp was invited to take some of the most solemn services. According to Irenaeus his ministry there was greatly blessed. It is obvious that the Bishop of Rome did not then claim any authority over other churches.

[1] See pp. 20 f.

Polycarp was burnt at Smyrna in the reign of the emperor Antoninus Pius. A letter from the church of Smyrna to the church of Philomelium dwells upon his kindness to his captors and his calm bearing at the stake. Most striking of all is his famous reply to the proconsul who offered to save his life if he would curse Christ. 'Eighty and six years have I served Him, and He hath done me no wrong; how then can I blaspheme my King who saved me?'[1]

Correspondence between Pliny and the emperor Trajan furnishes valuable information as to the position of the Church in the early years of the second century. When the former became governor of Bithynia (south of the Black Sea) in 111 A.D. he found that Christianity had progressed so much that the heathen temples were almost deserted. He was deeply concerned at the rapid spread of this 'depraved and extravagant superstition', and began taking steps to stop its advance. He seemed surprised, however, at the character of the Christians. He found that 'on an appointed day they had been accustomed to meet before daybreak, and to recite a hymn by turns to Christ, as to a god, and to bind themselves by an oath, not for the commission of any crime but to abstain from theft, robbery, adultery and breach of faith, and not to deny a deposit when it was claimed'. Although this is commonplace with Christians nowadays, it must have seemed to him, in that hard Roman world, an almost incredibly high plane of morality. Pliny consulted the emperor as to how he should deal with these people. His plan had been to ask in the first place if they were Christians. If they answered affirmatively, he repeated the question two or three times, threatening them with death.

Trajan's reply approved of the line taken by the governor. He ordered that no attention be paid to

---

[1] See 'Letter from the Church of Smyrna to Philomelium' (Eusebius, *Ecclesiastical History*, IV, chapter 15).

anonymous accusations, which lent themselves to abuse. Christians were not to be sought out for punishment. If they were openly informed against and the charge proved, they must be punished; but if they recanted and worshipped the pagan gods they were to be pardoned.

At first sight there seems to be little consolation for the Christians in this reply of Trajan. But in reality it brought considerable alleviation of their position, for it very much lessened the number of charges levelled against them.

The work of the early *Apologists* merits attention. The constant and widespread slanders against the Christians, and the misunderstanding of their position by the rulers, compelled them to write treatises, known as 'Apologies', defending their religion. The two earliest Apologists seem to have been Quadratus and Aristides in the first half of the second century. We know of their work only from the pages of Eusebius and even then the reference is very brief.

The greatest of the early Apologists was Justin Martyr, a most earnest Christian and a true lover of learning. He was born at Sychem in Palestine *c.* 100 A.D. and died as a martyr at Rome in 163 A.D. in the reign of Marcus Aurelius. His *First Apology* was addressed to the emperor Antonius Pius and the Senate, and the whole Roman people. The *Second Apology* is short and is to the Senate only. His lengthiest work is the *Dialogue with Trypho the Jew*, which aims at explaining the Christian faith to the Jews.

Justin's works reveal throughout a love of culture, a spirit of reverence, and an earnest desire to spread the knowledge of the faith. He was born a pagan and became a keen student of philosophy. He went from place to place earnestly seeking truth, visiting Rome, Athens, Alexandria and other important cities in his search. One day, walking near the shore at Ephesus, he met an old man 'of meek and venerable manners' who pointed him to the Scriptures and Jesus Christ. The flame of a divine love took possession of Justin, and he found the true philosophy.

In the *First Apology*, he refutes in a masterly fashion the usual charges against the Christians—their supposed atheism, their alleged disloyalty, their licentiousness in secret meetings, their cannibalism. His attitude to the thought-systems of his day is of great interest. For him, philosophy, especially Platonism, was good as far as it went. He insists, however, that Christians are saved by the power of Jesus and not by knowledge and philosophy, excellent though these are. It is heart-warming to read his expositions of the Scriptures to show that 'Christ was delivered up for our transgressions, and bore the sins of many'.[1]

His account of the Christian weekly worship is worth attention: 'On the day called Sunday, all who live in cities or in the country gather together to one place, and the memoirs of the apostles (i.e. gospels) or the writings of the prophets are read, as long as time permits; then, when the reader has ceased, the president verbally instructs, and exhorts to the imitation of these good things. Then, we all rise together and pray, and when our prayer is ended, bread and wine and water are brought, and the president in like manner offers prayers and thanksgivings, according to his ability, and the people assent, saying Amen; and there is a distribution to each, and a participation of that over which thanks have been given.'[2]

We note the marked simplicity of this second-century service, the reading of the Holy Scriptures, the address by the president, and his prayers 'according to his ability' which shows that extempore prayer was still customary. We note also that the minister is called 'president', which shows that he was one of the brethren

[1] Cf. *First Apology*, chapters 50, 51, 52. *Dialogue with Trypho*, chapter 95. (English trans.: Ante-Nicene Library, Vol. II).
[2] *First Apology*, chapter 67.

chosen to preside and not a member of a priestly caste.

In 163 A.D., or soon after, Justin and several companions were sentenced to death at Rome by the bullying Prefect, Junius Rusticus. They were asked in a severe tone 'Do you suppose that you will rise again, and live for ever?' Justin's noble reply was 'I do not suppose it. I know it'.

Under Marcus Aurelius persecution raged for years. One of the worst outbreaks was in 177 A.D. at Lyons and Vienne, in Gaul. A numerous Greek colony had come from Asia Minor to the Rhone Valley where they had established a strong and virile church which was ministered to by men who came from their old homeland. Eusebius presents us with a terrible picture of the sufferings of the faithful in this church. The mobs, possessed of a Satanic spirit, committed shocking atrocities such as the murder of Bishop Pothinus, aged 90. The heroic witness of Blandina, a martyred slave girl, who was fragile of body and timid of spirit, can never be forgotten. Day after day she was subjected to every kind of torture but her tormentors could not compel her to deny her faith. She seemed clearly sustained by God, and even that diabolical crowd said, 'Never woman in our time suffered so much'. In the end she was butchered by an official.

EARLY HERESIES

Many heresies arose and flourished during the second century. No history would be complete without some consideration of them.

The Nazarenes

This name was at first given derisively to the whole Church. Later it was applied to the sect which carried on the tradition of the early Judaizers who caused Paul so much trouble. Before the destruction of Jerusalem in 70 A.D. the Jewish Christians fled across Jordan and found refuge at Pella. Their descendants clung tenaciously to their Jewish customs long after Jewish Christians had abandoned them. They scrupulously kept the Law of Moses, and carefully observed circumcision and the rabbinical rules as to the Jewish Sabbath. Their influence was never powerful, but they lingered on till at least the end of the fourth century.

The Ebionites

These resembled the Nazarenes in a number of ways but were much more extreme and desired to impose the Jewish Law on every Christian. They rejected all the writings of Paul, and, of the four Gospels, recognized only St. Matthew. From even this Gospel they cut out all references to the Saviour's miraculous conception and pre-existence. Like the Gnostics (see below), they believed that it was only at His baptism that Jesus became divine when the Spirit descended on Him. The Spirit, they said, left Him before His death, and so it was just an ordinary man who suffered on the cross.

Gnosticism

This was a heresy far more subtle and dangerous than any which had hitherto appeared. It became so widespread that by the beginning of the third century most of the more intellectual Christian congregations throughout the Roman Empire were, to some degree or other, infected by it. It took many forms and in the short space available it is exceedingly difficult to do more than indicate some of its main features.

Gnostics gave a version of Christ's work which was devoid of any real Christian content, and proceeded to work up a system which combined their very nebulous Christian ideas with elements taken freely from the mythologies of Greece, Egypt, Persia, and India, and from the philosophies and theosophies of these lands. The word Gnostic comes from the Greek word *gnōsis*, 'knowledge'. This knowledge, they claimed, was esoteric or secret, and could be possessed only by that section of men who are 'pneumatic' or spiritual—the superior people. There was another class made up of the 'psychic', those who cannot get beyond faith. The prophets and other good Jews belonged to this class which is inferior to those having 'gnosis'. The great mass of the human race are 'hylic' (i.e. subject to matter) and so they are in hopeless bondage to Satan and to their own lusts.

The Gnostics taught that, as matter was utterly and irretrievably evil, salvation consisted in overcoming it and eliminating it. This could never be done except by those who had 'gnosis' and practised asceticism, and this knowledge could come only to the 'pneumatic' class. To resist matter and overcome it they abstained from material enjoyments. They saw in God's best gifts sources of danger and rejected the most innocent enjoyments for fear of contamination with what was material. On this ground their morals were at first exceedingly strict but, as so often happens when men live unnatural lives in contravention of the deepest cravings of their nature, they not seldom degenerated into shocking licentiousness and libertinism.

The two most brilliant Gnostic teachers were Valentinus and Basilides—both connected with Alexandria in the second century. Another leading figure was Marcion of Sinope who died at Rome in 170 A.D. He was an earnest man and approximated to the orthodox Christian position in some respects. He rejected, however, the Old Testament and taught that the God of the Old Testament was not the Father of the Lord Jesus Christ. He was excommunicated; but his purity of life and his sincerity gathered around him many followers.

According to the Gnostics the Supreme Being is self-existent, infinitely remote, and unknowable. He is the First Principle but without attributes, and is beyond time and change. The problem for them was how this ineffable Being, whom they called Bythos, could create

matter which they regarded as evil, or have anything to
do with it. They got over the difficulty by postulating
a series of thirty emanations from Bythos, each emana-
tion originating the next in order. When one of these
was sufficiently distant on the borderland of light and
darkness, he created the world and did it badly. This
was the Demiurge or God of the Old Testament who
was worshipped by the Jews.

All the Gnostic systems were wildly imaginative and
speculative, and exceedingly complex, and do not lend
themselves to treatment in a short work such as this. At
least one Gnostic school of thought which claimed to
be Christian, turned the Scriptures upside down, taught
that Pharaoh and Ahab were saints while Moses and
Elijah were sinners, and even regarded the God of the
Old Testament as very evil.

Some Gnostics wrote commentaries on the Bible and
this stimulated Christian scholars to study the criticism
of the Scriptures more carefully and led to the writing
of able treatises in defence of the faith. On the other
hand, Gnosticism greatly fostered asceticism which was
an importation from the East, and so the way was paved
for the rise of monasticism in the Church.

Montanism

At the time when Montanism arose, things were not
well with the Church. Gnosticism was offering a serious
challenge and undermining the foundations of Christianity. The apostles were all dead, and the remarkable
gifts of the Holy Spirit which characterized the early
Church were dying out. Many false prophets had
arisen, and prophecy itself was falling under suspicion.
The Church was settling down to an easy formalism.
The pulsating spiritual life of an earlier day was lacking,
and rigidity, if not frigidity, was becoming the order
of the day. Montanism arose as a strong reaction against
all this, and, particularly, against Gnosticism. There
was a clamant need for its witness to the fact of the

dependence of the Church on the Holy Spirit but, unfortunately, Montanism too, like the Gnosticism it criticized, fell into the temptation of placing human speculation above divine revelation.

This striking movement was started by Montanus a native of Ardabau in Mysia. He claimed to have received a special revelation from the Holy Spirit, and started a wild and frenzied revival campaign. He was joined by two rich ladies who had deserted their husbands. In some aspects of their teaching the Montanists remind us of the followers of Edward Irving in Britain last century, and of the Nazarenes and the Pentecostalists in America in our own day. They also professed to have authority to impose a more rigid discipline on the Church, forbade second marriages, and stressed the superiority of the celibate to the married state. In their pride, they thought they surpassed even Christ in their teaching. The accession of Tertullian of Carthage to their ranks was a great triumph for them. Nevertheless the sect disappeared from Africa by 370 A.D., and from other places by the beginning of the sixth century.

The Montanists were severe in their church discipline, dividing sins into remissible and irremissible—sins which could be forgiven, and those which could not be forgiven in this world. This reminds us of the distinction made later by the Roman Catholic Church between venial and mortal sins, although the list of sins was not quite the same. The extremism of Montanism produced some violent reactions. Because of the vivid descriptions given by them of a millennial epoch of sensuous enjoyment, the doctrine of Christ's Second Coming, with which this was identified, was laid aside by the Church as a whole. Once prophetism was discredited, Christ came to be regarded as far away, and the clergy were conceived of as having His affairs in their hands, and doing His work on earth through the Sacraments. This led to the exaltation of the ministers of the Church. Especially after the time of Cyprian, they were regarded as priests offering again the sacrifice of Christ at the altar.

The Montanists had also brought impassioned preaching into disrepute, together with all forms of emotionalism in religion. Preaching virtually ceased for many centuries. A direct result of this was that the priest was magnified because he ministered the awe-inspiring mysteries of the altar and it was supposed that only through him could men do business with God. Outside of the Church where he ministered there was no salvation. It was a sad departure from the faith of the apostolic Church, even though the priests vociferously claimed to be in the apostolic succession.

CHAPTER III

THE EARLY CATHOLIC FATHERS (180-250)

B Y the last quarter of the second century the position of the Church had been sadly undermined by
the cultured and heretical Gnostics, on the one
hand, with their fanciful speculations, and by the Montanists, on the other, with their dislike of learning and
their fanatical extremism which largely nullified what
was good in them. Spiritually, the Church had become
weak. It was just at this time that the Catholic Fathers
began their notable work. They were a truly remarkable group of most brilliant and devoted men—Irenaeus, Tertullian, Cyprian, Clement of Alexandria and
Origen. Three great difficulties confronted them. They
tackled them with considerable determination, but
some of their solutions raised up grave problems for
later ages.

1. *The New Testament Canon*

The list of books to be accepted into the Canon of the
New Testament was not absolutely fixed. The Gnostics put forward Gospels and Epistles of their own and
demanded their acceptance. Many of these were fan-
tastic and mischievous, and the problem was how to
find a standard of truth which would be accepted by
all. Irenaeus stressed that the real test was whether
the books were by the apostles, or at least by men
closely connected with them. Those which were apostolic, in this sense, were called 'Scriptures' by Irenaeus; and a little later we find Tertullian writing of

the 'New Testament' which he placed on a level with
the Old as regards divine inspiration.

2. *The rule of faith*

The Gnostics were difficult to argue with, not only
because they used spurious Gospels and Epistles, but
because, with their allegorical method of interpretation, they could make even the genuine Scriptures
appear to bear any meaning they wished. To protect the
Church from this sort of thing candidates for baptism
were asked to accept from an early period a certain
simple creed, or rule of faith. Thus grew up what we
now call the Apostles' Creed. Irenaeus appealed to the
doctrinal beliefs of the various churches which dated
back to the days of the apostles, to find a true credal
basis. He appealed to the 'tradition' of these churches
to find the true doctrine.[1] This served its purpose then,
but afterwards became a serious stumbling-block as
people got farther away from apostolic times and
traditions became vague and unreliable.

3. *Apostolic succession*

Irenaeus also appealed to the idea of an apostolic succession of office-bearers in the Church. These were
viewed as guarding the sacred deposit of the faith
which had been given through the apostles, and the
tradition which reached back to the days of the apostles. Lists were made of the succession of bishops in
the larger churches. It is noticeable, however, that
Irenaeus, like the early Church, makes no distinction
between 'bishops' and 'presbyters'. For example, he
refers sometimes to Polycarp as 'bishop', sometimes as
'presbyter'. He deals similarly with the whole list of
bishops at Rome. The presbyter (or elder) was by now,
however, imperceptibly passing into a bishop in more
or less the modern sense. When we come to Tertullian
and Clement in the third century, the transition has

[1] Irenaeus, *Against Heresies*, III, chapter 4.

been made. The Church has come to find its unity in the episcopate, and now appeals to the supposed 'tradition' which has come down through the bishops. This subsequently led to the undue prominence given by the Roman Catholic Church to tradition, which resulted in their placing it side by side with the Holy Scriptures.

IRENAEUS OF GAUL

Irenaeus, the first of the great Fathers, or teachers, of the period 180-250, was born in the province of Asia about 130. He was a disciple of Polycarp of Smyrna who was, in turn, a disciple of St. John. Thus, at the end of the second century, he was only at one remove from those who knew directly one or more of the apostles, and was, therefore, in a unique position to appeal to tradition in his arguments with the Gnostics, for the lives of St. John, Polycarp, and himself covered between them about 200 years. The tradition, therefore, was likely at this stage to be reliable.

We read of Irenaeus as being at Lyons in Gaul in 177. After the brutal murder by the mob of the aged Pothinus in that year, he was called to succeed him as bishop. His greatest service to the Church of God was through his extensive writings. We still have his work *Against Heresies* in five books. The importance of this work in saving the Church from the insidious and pernicious doctrines of the Gnostics cannot be exaggerated.

TERTULLIAN OF CARTHAGE

There is nothing to show when the gospel was first carried to North Africa. All at once in 180 there appears on the page of history a strong, vigorous Church, with its members suffering martyrdom fearlessly in the remote communities of Madaura[1] and

[1] See B. J. Kidd, *A History of the Church*, 1, pp. 251f.; H. M. Gwatkin, *Early Church History*, 1, pp. 167f.

Scilla. Tertullian, Cyprian and Augustine were all members of this Church, and left an indelible impression on the ages which came after them. Here, the first Latin Christian literature was developed, for Carthage, a large and beautiful city, was pre-eminently a centre of Latin culture.

It was in Carthage that Tertullian was born between 155 and 160. His parents were pagans and he lived the usual life of cultured pagans in that city of corrupt theatres and brutal gladiatorial contests. He was trained as a lawyer; this naturally had a great effect upon his manner of expressing theological concepts and later influenced deeply the forms of thought and the theological terms of the Church as a whole. He was the first to use the term *Trinity* in writing of the Godhead.

The church at Carthage and the church at Alexandria represented opposite tendencies. The one distrusted philosophy and emphasized Christian dogma; the other loved philosophy and liked to speculate and express theological ideas in philosophical terms.

We feel amazed as we contemplate the energy, dash and daring of Tertullian. His brilliant forensic gifts were used to the utmost in defence of Christianity. His courage was unlimited and he attacked with vigour and invective the highest authorities in the Empire. His writings were voluminous, and thirty treatises besides other works have come down to us. His *Apology* written in 197, in the reign of Septimius Severus, is perhaps the ablest ever written. As a great lawyer he brings out with crushing effect points never dealt with by other Christian Apologists. In his *De Idolatria* he discusses questions such as: What should a Christian do when invited by a pagan neighbour to a wedding or other social event where some pagan rite may be performed? He maintains that a Christian could not enter the army or hold public office because he would be called on to participate in heathen rites, such as pouring out libations.

A book which had very far-reaching and mischievous effects was his *De Praescriptione*. It was aimed at the Gnostics and other heretics. Tertullian fell back on a practice of the law courts—to raise a 'prescription' or preliminary objection which cut off the opponent at the beginning. Tertullian cuts off the heretics by insisting that the churches founded by the apostles have the deposit of truth. They, and they alone, have the correct tradition. Hence, the Church should not admit heretics to discussions on the Scriptures. The door is thus slammed in their faces.

This was dangerous doctrine, and led to much ecclesiastical despotism and intolerance in later ages. He falsely assumed that tradition must be in accordance with, and therefore equal with, Scripture, and developed the views of Irenaeus on this subject. From this there was evolved, in due time, the full Roman Catholic doctrine of Church authority and tradition.

Tertullian, like Irenaeus, held to the teaching of Paul in Romans v that in our first head, Adam, all men sinned and fell, and that in Christ, the second Adam, believers are redeemed from all evil. The point he dwelt upon most, however, was the inherited sinfulness of the human race. His thoughts on this theme were very suggestive and prepared the way for Augustine's profound treatment of the subject of sin and grace. Tertullian, however, fell far short of Augustine in this field, for while he regarded grace as opposed to nature, he did not regard it as opposed to merits, and so he opened the way for a doctrine of salvation by 'good works', at least in part.

He favoured very rigid penance in the Church, was very ascetic in his outlook and utterly condemned second marriages. He regarded military service in a pagan State as quite inconsistent with the Christian life and, because of the prevailing immorality, condemned in the strongest terms attendance at the theatre and at public amusements. For a man with his stern, gloomy, passionate nature, Montanism was congenial, and it is not strange that in his later years he joined this sect. In spite of this, his great gifts continued to secure for him the respect of the Church generally. He had, however, grave faults, and could be unfair, fanatical and vindictive.

CYPRIAN OF CARTHAGE

Cyprian is important not only for his strong emphasis on tradition, in which he resembled Tertullian, but because he brought forward far-reaching claims for the episcopate, and also introduced sacerdotal conceptions which brought about revolutionary changes in the worship of the Church. He was born at Carthage about 200 A.D. of cultured, noble and wealthy parents. When 46 years of age he was won to Christ by an aged presbyter whom he had befriended, and who directed him to the study of the Bible. He then sold his beautiful estate in literal obedience to the words of Christ and gave the money to the poor. He was baptized, and two years later became a presbyter. Very soon afterwards he was elected Bishop of Carthage by popular acclamation. He did not want to take so high a post but the people insisted and he felt it was a revelation of the divine will. This election by the people of such a recent convert aroused bitter feelings among presbyters who were passed over, and this led to schism.

In the year 250, under the emperor Decius, a persecution began which was more severe than any which had preceded it and which decimated the Church. It sifted out the unfaithful, nominal Christians, of which there were now many, and left the loyal and robust members to carry on a witness to the gospel. Cyprian had to withdraw from Carthage but returned in 251. He is important in church history for the following reasons:

1. *His strenuous insistence on the high place of the episcopate.* This originated in the considerable opposition from schismatics which he had to face. In Carthage, opponents led by Novatus set up a rival bishop. This party, supported by the 'confessors', as those honoured by the Church for enduring persecution were called, wanted a relaxation in ecclesiastical discipline and wished to receive back into church membership, without any proof of repentance, those who had denied Christ in the day of trial and made shipwreck of their faith. The party of Novatian (a rival bishop at Rome) stood for extreme severity in discipline, and insisted that no one who had denied the faith, or been guilty of a 'deadly' sin should ever be restored again to church membership. Cyprian encountered very strong opposition from both sides. To meet it, he insisted on the unity of the Church and denounced the sin of not rendering obedience to the bishop, who had, he said, his authority direct from God. He made the most stupendous claims for the absolute supremacy of the bishop as a God-appointed ruler of the Church. In succeeding ages this claim was accepted far and wide, and as a result church government became almost completely autocratic.

2. *His concept of the clergy as sacrificing priests.* He was the first to give this idea concrete shape in the Christian Church. The Lord's Supper he regarded as the offering up on the altar of the very body and blood of Christ. The change was serious and led in time to the doctrine of Transubstantiation and the abuses of the sacrifice of the Mass. Until Cyprian's time the Church constantly boasted in its dealing with pagans that it had neither altar nor sacrifice.

3. *His strong belief in the autonomy of each bishop in his own church.* Bishop Stephen of Rome, finding that he could not bring all the churches to agree with him as to the baptism of heretics, sent forth a despotic decree demanding submission from the other churches,

especially those at Carthage and in Asia, which opposed
him. Cyprian rose in his strength and did battle against
the usurpation of Rome, as Polycarp and Irenaeus had
done before him.

In 258, in the Valerian persecution, Cyprian was
beheaded forty miles from Carthage. The great multitude which looked on, and which included many
pagans, was deeply moved at the faith and courage
which he displayed.

From Carthage we turn to Alexandria. Founded by
Alexander the Great in 332 B.C., it became one of the
greatest cities in the world, with a population of
possibly two-and-a-half million people. There was no
more cosmopolitan city anywhere. Its commerce was
vast, for it did business with all the nations from India
to the Atlantic. Its culture was Greek, and second only
to that of Athens. Its illustrious men were many. In
this city, about 200 B.C., the Septuagint, or Greek
version of the Old Testament, which prepared the way
for the gospel among Greek-speaking people, had
been made. The monotheism of the large Jewish population, Platonism, Neo-Platonism, and Gnosticism, all
affected the life of thinking men in Alexandria.

In the second and third centuries A.D. the Church in
this great city produced a series of outstanding leaders, men like Pantaenus, Clement, and Origen. The
Catechetical School, over which these Christian teachers presided in turn, came to be very highly regarded,
not only for its theology but also for its philosophy
and science. It had been founded because they realized
that in these spheres the Church must face up to the
world of learning around them. At first it was intended
only for catechumens, but it soon established courses
in philosophy, grammar, literature, mathematics, and
science. Crowds of students flocked to this centre of
learning. They came not only from among the Christians but from among those pagans who were earnestly

seeking for the truth. Pantaenus, Clement, and Origen were men of noble Christian character. Surrounded by a restless intellectual community, and living in a very cosmopolitan city notorious for its turbulence, they all suffered much for the faith and were ready to die for it if need be, so great was their love to Christ.

CLEMENT

Clement became head of the school about 190. Unlike Tertullian, he considered that pagan philosophy could not be ignored by the Christian Church. He maintained that it had elements of great value but held, at the same time, that all true learning was given by God to lead men at last to the Holy Scriptures where we have the final revelation of Himself. Clement aimed at gathering in the treasures of wisdom and knowledge from all sources and using them for Christ. He was driven from Alexandria in 202 in the fierce persecution under Septimius Severus. He died in 220 in Caesarea. His extensive works included *Hortatory Address to the Greeks, The Instructor,* and a large collection of *Miscellanies.*

ORIGEN

Origen (185-254) was one of the most brilliant teachers and writers ever known in the Christian Church. The son of a martyr, and reared in a fine spiritual atmosphere, he became head of the Catechetical School at the age of 18 and raised it to its highest fame in spite of persecution. He loved the Scriptures and showed remarkable ability in interpreting them. He went to considerable extremes in his asceticism—fasting, refusing wine and all delicate food, and sleeping on the bare floor. He toiled incessantly and, according to Jerome, 'Produced more books than any other man could read in a lifetime'. Some estimated his works at 6,000, including letters and articles. His best known books are the *Hexapla,* his voluminous *Com-*

mentaries, First Principles (the first work on systematic theology), and *Against Celsus,* a most brilliant apologetic treatise.

While believing strongly in the divine inspiration of the Scriptures, he fell into the snare of allegoric interpretation so typical of Alexandria. He stressed the deity of Christ and the doctrine of the Trinity as against various heretical schools, which resembled somewhat our modern Unitarians. He saw that the doctrinal questions at issue were of vast importance, especially that which concerned the true divinity of our Lord. The early Church had regarded Christ as unquestionably Lord and God. He was adored with a simple reverence, and believers did not speculate as to the mode of His divine being or the relationship between His deity and humanity. From the end of the second century, however, new theories began to present themselves, the chief of which was Monarchianism. This word meant for the Greek theologians that there was only one Person in the Godhead. The names Father, Son, and Holy Spirit could be applied indiscriminately to this one Person. Two views prevailed as regards the nature of Christ:

1. Some believed that a divine power descended on the man Jesus and enabled Him to do the works of God. This was *dynamistic Monarchianism,* from the Greek word *dunamis,* power. This view was maintained by Theodotus, Artemon, and Paul of Samosata, as well as by the Alogi who denied the Logos teaching of St. John.

2. The other belief was that all the fulness of God dwelt in Christ and that this was a *mode* of God's manifestation. Hence the system was called *modalistic Monarchianism.* Sometimes God manifested Himself as the Father, sometimes as the Son, and at other times as the Holy Spirit, but it was always the same divine Person although differently manifested. Praxeas, Noetus, Beryllus, and Sabellius took this view. The

last mentioned was the best known and his name is often given to Monarchianism in general, although there were minor differences between him and the other exponents of the heresy. The Monarchian theory was severely criticized because it implied that the eternal Father had suffered on the cross. On this account its supporters were called *Patripassians*. The teaching of Scripture, accepted by the Church catholic, was that Christ was truly God and that at the same time He had a personality distinct from the Father and the Holy Spirit, and yet was one with Them. Origen rendered invaluable service in his powerful and clear defence of this great article of the faith. In particular his exposition of the doctrine of the Son's eternal generation paved the way, in 325, for the decision of the Council of Nicea as to Christ's deity, as well as for later pronouncements in the ecumenical councils of the fourth century.

In the field of speculation, Origen's imagination ran riot. He claimed that he was loyal to the rule of faith adopted by the Church, while exercising ample liberty of expression on matters not covered by the accepted creed. His bold, pioneering spirit caused him to be regarded as a heretic in many quarters. His theory about the successive incarnations of the human soul illustrates how freely he could speculate on what he thought was an open question. It is, he said, of the very nature of God to be ever creating. There must have been a series of created worlds, and souls must have been created from the beginning. The unequal state of men, angels, and devils now must be due to their experiences in the various worlds they have been in; for all at first must have been equal because God is just. Souls are always rising or falling. They go up or down as a reward or punishment for their actions in each successive state of existence. Even the devil himself can yet ascend to higher worlds. Punishment, he believed, is purely remedial, and, finally, in the long cycle of the ages, every soul must be gathered home to the bosom of the divine Father. Those who taught in the nineteenth century the doctrine of the 'larger hope' were following, with faltering steps, the trail blazed by Origen.

Bishop Demetrius of Alexandria became very jealous of his brilliant subordinate and had him excommunicated and exiled after he had been for twenty-eight years the distinguished head of the Catechetical School. At Caesarea in Palestine he established another centre of learning and for twenty years more he continued to influence all grades of society. He was thrown into prison at Tyre during the Decian persecution, and was broken down by his terrible suffering there, and died soon after his release in 254.

CHAPTER IV

TRIAL AND TRIUMPH

IN the reigns of Alexander Severus (222-235) and Philip the Arabian (244-249), the Church was treated by the civil power in a friendly way. It was a period of syncretism, when men were trying to find a common faith by extracting the best from all religions. Origen kept up a friendly correspondence with Philip, and for thirty-eight years the Church was left in peace. As a result it greatly increased in numbers and prestige. But then came the terrible persecutions under Decius and Valerian which continued, with some intervals of relaxation, from 250 to 260.

This period was a time of great calamity for the Empire. The barbarians were pressing in on all sides. The invasions by the Goths were specially serious. Decius (249-251) believed that safety lay only in reviving the ancient virtues of the Roman people, and decided therefore that Christianity must be rooted out. In the reign of Valerian (254-260) the political situation became still more perilous. The emperor was persuaded to renew the persecution, which, once begun, was systematic and terrible. Some of the outstanding victims were Cyprian of Carthage, and two bishops of Rome, Stephen and Sixtus II.

After the Valerian persecution the Church was allowed to go unmolested for over forty years. Before the end of the century there were Christians in every sphere of life, and for eighteen years Diocletian, who succeeded to the throne in the East in 284, refrained from any persecution because it might bring down the Empire. At last, however, he was persuaded by Galerius, his relentless colleague in the East, to begin the most ruthless of all attempts to stamp out the Church. It began in 303 with an edict to destroy Christian places of worship, and all the sacred books of the Christians. When the prefect and his men entered the large and beautiful church at Nicomedia, the capital of the Eastern part of the Empire, they were amazed to find no image of the deity. They burnt the Holy Scriptures, pillaged what they wanted, and razed the building to the ground.

In the region administered under Diocletian by Galerius, the persecution was especially brutal, with scourging and tortures before death. The Western emperor, Maximian, also carried out the edicts with full force in Italy and Africa. Constantius, however, the 'Caesar' under Maximian of Gaul, Britain, and Spain, refused to inflict death on anyone for his religion, maintaining that 'the temple of God', the human body, must not be so maltreated. He continued this policy even when he and Galerius succeeded Maximian and Diocletian as emperors in 305.

In 306, Constantius died and was succeeded by his son Constantine who marched victoriously against several rival claimants to the throne. Before the battle of the Milvian Bridge, October 27, 312, when he defeated Maxentius, he passed through a remarkable spiritual experience. The story goes that he saw in the sky a flaming cross with the inscription in Greek, 'By this sign conquer.' Whether this was an optical illusion due to his excitement at the time, it is hard to say. The whole incident may just be pious legend. What is certain is that something affected him profoundly. Whilst his motives were sometimes mixed and he retained some old superstitions, he now showed that he fervently believed in the God of the Christians.

This conversion of the emperor was an event of surpassing importance to the Church, for not only was it productive of great good, but it led also to certain evils. Only a few years earlier such an occurrence would have been regarded as quite impossible. In 312 Constantine had become joint-emperor with Licinius. A few months later, in March 313, they issued from Milan their epoch-making decree giving full toleration to the Christian faith, and restoring to the Church all places of worship which had been confiscated, and making good all losses. This was indeed an historic day. A notable fact about this proclamation is that it was based upon the rights of the individual conscience, and granted unconditional religious liberty to all in the West, a truly remarkable decision in such an age. Eleven years later Constantine, having quarrelled with Licinius, defeated him in battle at Adrianople and became master of the whole Empire, East and West. Christianity now enjoyed complete freedom throughout the Roman world. With his growing power, Constantine became more vain and self-complacent. He himself liked to be arrayed in splendid robes. It is not surprising, therefore, to find him presenting the bishop of Jerusalem with a set which vied in splendour with the best vestments of the pagan high priests. This is the first instance of the use of vestments in the Christian Church.

The emperor maintained close friendship with the bishops and did his best to settle the various controversies which arose in the Church at this time. This led to an intervention by the State in Church affairs and created a precedent which proved a most serious problem in later ages. There were, however, very solid advantages as well. They are seen, for example, in the greatly improved status of women, in the mitigation of the horrors of slavery, and in the keeping of the Lord's Day for rest and worship. At the same time, the favours of the State, welcome though they were, tended to produce an arrogant spirit in the clergy.

Constantine's successors were by no means equal to himself in either character or ability. His sons had troubled reigns, and, for the most part, favoured Arianism[1]. His grandson, Julian the Apostate (361-363), because of the evil treatment meted out to him by the sons of Constantine and the massacre of his relatives by them, renounced Christianity and did his best to restore a reformed kind of paganism. Polytheism was, however, rotten to the core and the attempts to restore it proved a fiasco.

At the beginning of this fourth century Christianity, as we have seen, had suffered, under Diocletian, the greatest of all persecutions; but by its end paganism had virtually disappeared in the Roman Empire. Jerome could declare in his time that every heathen altar in Rome was forsaken and every temple desolate. Yet, in the Christian Church itself there were at work tendencies towards priestcraft, sacramentarianism, and monasticism which were ominous for the future.

[1] See pp. 53ff.

CHAPTER V

GREAT COUNCILS, GREAT MEN.
GREAT EVENTS (325-500)

WE enter now a period of bitter theological controversy. The time had come for the Church
to clarify its attitude to certain great doctrinal
questions. The points at issue were thoroughly debated
in gatherings attended by the majority of Church
leaders, and the decisions of the first four Ecumenical
Councils, as they are called, were embodied in Creeds
which are still accepted, at least nominally, by the
Christian churches. It was a peculiarly turbulent age
in the theological sphere. In the fifth century, in
particular, it was not uncommon for opposing parties
to seek victory by physical force, and shameful fights
ensued. Many unworthy things were said and done;
yet, out of all the strife, there emerged declarations of
faith which were of priceless value for succeeding
generations.

THE ARIAN CONTROVERSY

This controversy split the Church for a time and had
repercussions which were felt for about three centuries. Arius, who originated the dispute, was a presbyter in Alexandria. About the year 318 he began to
propagate views as to the divinity of Christ which
were contrary to the accepted doctrine of the Church.
He taught that Christ 'had come into being out of non-
existence'; that 'once He was not'; and that 'He was
created and made'.[1] On this view, the Son was inferior

[1] Sozomen, *Historia Ecclesiastica*, i, chapter 15, para. 3.

to the Father in nature and dignity although the first and noblest of all created beings. Alexander, the Bishop of Alexandria, took action in 320 and declared that he believed the Son to be 'consubstantial and co-eternal with the Father'. Arius was not straightforward in his controversial methods and cleverly tried to cloud the issues. He was deposed in 321, but being an able and charming man he was befriended by eminent ecclesiastics like Macarius, Bishop of Jerusalem, Eusebius of Nicomedia, and Eusebius of Caesarea, the historian.

Every effort at reconciliation between Bishop Alexander and Arius having failed, the emperor Constantine in 324 called the *First General Council* at Nicea, in north-west Asia Minor, to deal with the situation. This Ecumenical Council was attended by 318 bishops from most of the lands from Spain to Persia. It was, in truth, a remarkable gathering with the emperor in attendance and a fine Christian, Hosius of Cordoba, presiding. Many of those present bore the scars of persecution, with maimed limbs and blinded eyes. They had known the deepest suffering for Christ's sake, and now the emperor himself welcomed them. It was, indeed, a new epoch.[1]

The discussion resolved itself into a debate on the question whether Christ was 'Homousios' (i.e. of the same essence as God), or 'Homoiousios' (of similar essence with God). The chief protagonists were *Athanasius* (a deacon) and Arius who was, as we have seen, a presbyter. These, and not the bishops, were the men who really counted in the Council. At first many sought to procure a vague pronouncement which would commit them to neither side. In the end the orthodox party secured a large majority and the Council declared that Christ was 'the Son of God, only begotten of the Father . . . of the substance of the Father . . . very God of very God'. This decision has

[1] Eusebius, *Ecclesiastical History*, I, chapters 6, 7.

been of immeasurable importance in the history of the Church.

Arius was anathematized and banished with two companions to Illyria. Two years later, however, the strife was renewed in all its bitterness when Constantine received Arius back into favour, and banished Athanasius, now Bishop of Alexandria, to Treves when he refused to reinstate him. No less than five times was Athanasius exiled to distant regions and then recalled; and each time he returned to Alexandria he was received with delirious joy by his devoted flock. The intrigues of the Arians were innumerable. Often it was a case of 'Athanasius against the world, and the whole world against Athanasius'. After having known suffering and exile for the greater part of his active life, his last six years (367-373) were spent in peace and honour in his diocese of Alexandria.

The Council of Constantinople in 381 was the Second General Council, and was attended by 186 bishops. It emphatically asserted the deity of the Holy Spirit as against the views of Macedonius and Sabellius. The latter taught a kind of Unitarianism.[1]

The Council of Ephesus (in 431) condemned and deposed Nestorius, the eloquent Bishop of Constantinople, who in his opposition to the Monophysites so stressed the two natures of Christ that he was accused of teaching that Christ was two Persons. Monophysitism held that our Lord had one nature only, the divine having absorbed the human. One result of the growing stress on celibacy in the Church, was an insistence on the perpetual virginity of the Virgin Mary. To glorify her, she was given the title *Theotokos,* 'the Mother of God'. With good reason Nestorius protested, maintaining that Mary was mother of 'the Man, Christ Jesus', but not of His deity. The Council was glaringly unjust, and Nestorius was banished to the desert of the Thebaid. He had many followers in Syria

[1] See pp. 46 f.

and Persia, and they formed the Nestorian Church. In its early days this Church expanded remarkably rapidly. It established itself strongly first in Persia and then in Armenia. Its missionaries then pressed on further eastward and by 625 had reached China by way of Central Asia, a most honourable record. This Church still exists in Mesopotamia and Armenia in spite of terrible persecutions from the Muslims. Twenty years later Eutyches, the implacable opponent of Nestorius in the Council of Ephesus, was charged, to his great astonishment, with being himself a heretic, and with teaching that Christ had only one nature— the divine. Though defended by the turbulent Synod of Ephesus in 449 (known as the 'Robber' because of its injustice), he was condemned at the *Council of Chalcedon*. This Council, with an attendance of 500 bishops, affirmed that Christ has 'two natures inconfusedly, unchangeably' but which are united in one Person. To this day the opposite doctrine of One Nature ('Monophysitism') lingers on among the Jacobites of Syria, and the Copts of Egypt and Abyssinia.

OUTSTANDING CHURCHMEN

The references to these must be very brief but even to know their names and their periods is of some value.

1. *Hilary of Poitiers* (295-368) stands out as the great champion of orthodoxy in the West as against the Arians of his time. His theological writings were many and very able.

2. *Ambrose of Milan* (340-397) was, in character, one of the most unbending men ever known. His courage never failed and he withstood the strongest rulers. He would not allow the setting aside of any place of worship in Milan for the Arians even when this was demanded by the mother of the emperor Valentinian II. Later, he not only refused communion to Maximus who had usurped the throne of the Western Empire,

but even to the great emperor Theodosius who was denied admission to church for eight months after he had ordered a massacre of rebels in Thessalonica. The emperor made a complete capitulation.

3. *Aurelius Augustine* (354-430) is so important that he must receive fuller treatment than others. He was born at Tagaste in Numidia, his father being then a coarse pagan, while his mother, Monica, was a Christian of outstanding saintliness. To her self-sacrifice, noble faith, and incessant prayers, Augustine owed more than can be estimated. His *Confessions* form a classic of self-revelation and show the sensuality of his early years among the licentious students of Carthage. At 17 he took a young woman as a concubine. When a son was born, he called him Adeodatus ('by God given'), a strange name in the circumstances.

He was influenced successively by the *Hortensius* of Cicero, the Bible, the Manichaeans, Aristotle, and the New Platonism. For years he prayed 'O God, grant me chastity and continence, but not yet'. Then, at Milan, where he was holding a post as government teacher of Rhetoric, he fell under the spell of the great bishop, Ambrose. Finally, his internal conflict became intolerable, and under a fig tree in the garden, in a paroxysm of weeping, he found the Saviour of whom his mother had so often told him. The spiritual change was complete. He knew it was all from the sovereign mercy of God, and henceforth, like Paul, the marvels of divine grace became his chief theme.

In 395 he was made Bishop of Hippo in North Africa, a place to which his name gives lustre still. His fertile brain brought forth book after book, such as *De Vita Beata*; *De Ordine*; and *De Baptismo*. His most notable works were on sin and grace and were called forth by the Pelagian Controversy in 412, when Pelagius, a British monk, denied original sin and refused to believe that the sinner was helpless to save himself. Augustine insisted that sin wrought such ravages in man that he cannot save himself. He maintained that no man can really love God or believe in Him savingly until the grace of God comes to him. These teachings profoundly affected both Luther and Calvin at the Reformation. According to Rudolf Eucken, the great apologetical treatise *The City of God* entitles Augustine to be regarded 'as the one great philosopher sprung from the soil of Christianity proper'. He died in 430 while the barbarian Vandals were besieging his beloved city of Hippo.

Augustine was the greatest Christian of his age; but he sanctioned certain beliefs and customs which were afterwards productive of much evil in the Church. Thus he taught that there was no salvation outside the visible Catholic Church (with its traditionalism and sacramentarianism). He also favoured ascetic monasticism, fostered the use of relics and encouraged belief in purgatory. Nevertheless, no other mind since the time of the apostles has made such a deep impression on Christian thought, whether Protestant, Roman Catholic, scholastic or mystic.

4. *The Three Cappadocians* is the name given to Basil the Great, Bishop of Caesarea in Cappadocia (329-379), his brother, Gregory of Nyssa (332-394), and their great friend Gregory of Nazianzus (330-390). They were men of the highest character, ready to devote themselves and their riches unreservedly to the cause of Christ. In the fourth century, when Arianism was strongly aided by the secular power and many theologians were unscrupulous in their attacks on those who supported the Nicene Creed, they stood out boldly in the Eastern Church in defence of the cause for which Athanasius had earlier suffered.

5. *John Chrysostom* (347-407), Bishop, first of Antioch and then of Constantinople, was a saintly man, an outstanding scholar, and one of the greatest orators of all time. (Hence his name, which means 'John of the golden mouth'.) His faithfulness in

preaching repentance offended the empress Eudoxia, and he was deposed and banished in 403. He died through ill-treatment on his way as a prisoner to Pityus on the Black Sea.

6. *Jerome* (340-420), one of the most interesting and picturesque figures in church history, was born in northern Dalmatia. He produced the Latin Vulgate Version of the Bible, which, even today, is the only version recognized as authentic by the Roman Church. He started a monastic community at Aquileia but it broke up in a 'whirlwind' of dissension. He was a man of hasty temper and never suffered fools gladly. Nevertheless, because of his scholarship and force of character, there was much that was attractive about him. He spent thirty-four years at Bethlehem, where he lived mostly in a cave as a hermit and carried out his immense literary and scholarly labours. He defended monasticism and celibacy with extravagant enthusiasm but found that the world always invaded even the loneliest retreats.

7. Leo I, known as *Leo the Great* (390-461), stands out as the first truly great churchman to appear in Rome since apostolic times. The Council of Chalcedon (451) agreed that the term 'pope' be reserved exclusively for him and his successors at Rome.[1] The personality of Leo made so great an impression upon the rough pagan conquerer, Attila, that he turned back from the gates of Rome at his behest. He was a man who bent all his strength towards gaining recognition for the Bishop of Rome as Universal Bishop. He based the claim on the primacy supposed to have been granted to Peter (Mt. xvi. 18). He gave a new interpretation to these words, a meaning which differed from that placed on them by Ambrose, Jerome, and Augustine. His claim was conceded in the West, with the excep-

---

[1] It is remarkable that, before Leo, only one Roman bishop could be regarded as really outstanding. This was Hippolytus (d. 235) who was bishop of a sect and much opposed to the official Roman bishops.

tion of the Celtic Church, and was strongly backed up by a decree from the emperor Valentian III who made it an offence against the State to resist the dictates of the pontiff. Leo took up the extraordinary attitude that 'Peter has never quitted the guidance of the Church which he received'.

The Church in the East emphatically repudiated his claims. Even the Council of Chalcedon, where he exercised much influence, refused his request to be recognized as Universal Bishop. His assertion of papal supremacy, however, produced a profound effect in later ages.

A CHANGING WORLD (400-500)

The fifth century is for ever memorable as the period when the Roman Empire fell before the barbarians of the north and north-east. Love of luxury, rural de-population, and other ills, had weakened the Empire. Little by little the Teutonic tribes had been pressing across the frontiers.

Alaric the Visigoth, after various victories and set-backs, entered Rome and sacked it in 410. At this dis-tance of time we cannot envisage all that this meant. Jerome in his cave at Bethlehem wept on receiving the tidings 'because she was a captive: that city which enthralled the world'. Multitudes felt the same. After a year Alaric died, and his successor, instead of ruling in his own name, accepted office nominally under Honorius, emperor of the West. But henceforth the power of the emperors was but a shadow of that formerly enjoyed. Most of the conquering barbarian tribes were Arian Christians. Although they were not orthodox, it was fortunate for the Church in the Roman Empire that their conquerors professed any kind of Christianity, for it saved many Christian lives and much church property, not only in Rome but else-where.

There is not space to follow in detail the devastating conquests of the barbarians, and to tell how Rome, 'the Empress of the World', finally fell; how Burgundians, Suevi, Vandals, and Alans pushed west, overrunning Gaul in 408; how Alaric, the West Goth, captured Rome in 410; how the Vandals, crossing over from Spain, ravaged the fertile province of Africa in 429; how Attila and his hordes of Huns were beaten at Chalons-sur-Marne in 451 by the army of Rome and the nations of Gaul; how Genseric and his Vandals crossed from Africa to Italy in 455 and plundered Rome; and how, at last, the 'eternal city' which had proudly ruled the nations for twelve centuries, fell before Odoacer, the Herulean, in 476, thus marking the end of an epoch.

The last of the Roman legions left Britain in 410 to defend Gaul and Italy. The Jutes, Angles, and Saxons, fierce pagans, poured across the North Sea from northern Germany, and destroyed the Christian Church in eastern England and south-eastern Scotland. The Celtic Church lived on in western Britain and Ireland and showed great vitality. Being separated from the Churches in Europe by the pagan belt established in the east of the country, it was preserved from much of the decline in spiritual fervour and culture which characterized continental Christianity during this period.

The Roman Empire of the West was now under barbarian dominion and broken up into various States. There ensued a period of no small uncertainty in these different countries as victors and vanquished, Catholics, Arians, and pagans all tried to settle down side by side. The old Roman culture had received a shattering blow, but the strong and virile Teutons brought with them a new vigour and a new vision to replace a civilization which had become effete. It was a difficult time for Christianity, and although the barbarians gradually became Catholic Christians (for example, in 496 Clovis, King of the Franks, was baptized with three thousand of his warriors), these accessions were by no means all gain to the Church. The spiritual tone was sadly lowered and many barbarian errors and superstitions found entry.

Contrary to what we might expect, the fall of the Roman Empire increased the personal prestige of the Bishop of Rome. When Alaric entered the city, most of the great patrician families fled. Some, for example, were welcomed in Palestine by Jerome. This left the bishop pre-eminent in the social life of the city, and his moral authority increased enormously as a result.

CHAPTER VI

THE BEGINNING OF THE MIDDLE AGES

AT the end of the sixth century a new order of things was emerging in Europe. The influence of the Graeco-Roman culture was lessening and at the same time new forms of thought were becoming predominant because of the intermingling of Teutonic and Roman ideas. The Middle Ages may well be taken as beginning in 590 when Gregory I ascended the papal throne. War and famine had decimated a great part of Italy. The Lombards, who had captured northern Italy in 568, were a menace to the Roman See. Outside Italy the prestige of the Catholic Church had not been regained since the fall of the Empire in 476. The regions of the Rhine and the Danube had been lost to the Church. Arianism and other heresies were rampant in the States formed by the barbarians. The influence of the Roman pontiff had become very weak in Spain, Gaul and Illyria, and had almost vanished in Africa.

The conversion in 496 of Clovis, the pagan king of the Franks, had not yet led to any great increase in the power of the pope, although that nation was destined to become the great bulwark of the See of Rome in the eighth and ninth centuries. The conversion of Recared the Visigoth king of Spain from Arianism to the Catholic faith in 589 was very encouraging, but there were still innumerable difficulties confronting the pontiff. It was a time when spiritual fires were burning low.

POPE GREGORY THE GREAT (590-604)

This was the state of affairs when Gregory became Bishop of Rome. His brilliant rule set a standard for those who came after him and he is really the first 'pope' who can, with perfect accuracy, be given this title. Along with Leo I (440-461), Gregory VII (1073-1085), and Innocent III (1198-1216), he stands out as one of the chief architects of the papal system which has influenced so greatly the history of the world.

Gregory was born about 540 in a rich, senatorial family in Rome, and early entered the imperial service, becoming, through sheer ability, Prefect of the city of Rome in 573. The exarch of Ravenna (representing the Eastern Emperor in Italy) either could not, or would not, help in the defence of the city against the Lombards. In the emergency, Gregory assumed the highest powers and justified his management of affairs by success in the political and military spheres as well as in the civic.

Hearing the call of God, he devoted himself to a religious life and sold his vast estates in 574, dedicating the proceeds to the welfare of the poor and to the building of six monasteries in Sicily. He became a monk of the Benedictine Order. In 579 Pope Pelagius II sent him on an embassy to Constantinople where he gained invaluable experience in diplomacy. In 586 he became abbot of his monastery in Rome, and in 590 was elected pope. Schaff very aptly sums up the character of Gregory as 'monastic, ascetic, devout, and superstitious; hierarchical, haughty, and ambitious, yet humble before God'.[1] His former experience in government service and diplomacy served him in good stead in negotiations with the Lombard rulers, and he became the most potent political force in Italy. He showed the same consummate ability in managing the vast papal estates near Rome in Calabria, Sicily,

[1] Philip Schaff, *Mediaeval Christianity*, I, p. 212.

Corsica, Dalmatia, Gaul and Africa, thus helping to lay the foundations for the temporal power of the Pope which was to become so important in international relationships at a later period.

Gregory bent his ceaseless energies towards increasing the prestige of his See in lands where it had fallen low, and his efforts were not in vain. He saw clearly the need for Missions, for more than two-thirds of Europe was still pagan, and it was he who conceived the idea of sending a Roman mission to the Anglo-Saxons of England. He sought to turn the 'other-worldliness' of the monks to practical account and sent them forth to evangelize the heathen.

The claim to universal supremacy in the Church, first made by Leo I, was renewed by Gregory on the same grounds. When in 588 John, the Patriarch of Constantinople, assumed the title of 'Universal Bishop', Gregory protested strongly to the emperor and to the patriarch himself that it was 'proud, profane, wicked, blasphemous', and suggested that the patriarch was 'the forerunner of Anti-Christ'. He himself assumed the title of 'Servant of servants' which is still borne by the popes; but Gregory's attitude seems somewhat ludicrous considering that he made for himself assumed the title of 'Servant of servants' which is Peter' and the 'Vicar of Christ on earth', which clearly implied supremacy over all the Church. He made this claim very specifically. It was recognized almost everywhere in the West, the Celtic Church being again a notable exception. Even the East granted him a certain 'primacy of honour', although not of episcopal authority. Like Augustine, he taught that there was no salvation for anyone outside the one Catholic Church, and he claimed to be the head of it.

He was a man of deeply devotional spirit who regarded the Holy Scriptures with profound respect and looked for the speedy coming of the Lord to judge a wicked world. He was long remembered as a powerful preacher and an able theological writer. The doctrine of purgatory, which others had adumbrated since the days of Origen, was now officially promulgated by Gregory. The Gregorian chant seems to have been developed later, and his influence on music and ritual was not so great as was at one time supposed; but he encouraged the use of pictures and images in church on condition that they would not be worshipped. Gregory strengthened the Roman Church remarkably in a difficult period, and helped to secure for his successors that predominance for which he himself strove with might and main.

THE CHRISTIANIZATION OF BRITAIN

The fact that in 596 Pope Gregory sent his friend and brother monk, Augustin, from Rome to Christianize the Anglo-Saxons in England, is well known. It is not so well known that in Roman times, by the end of the third century in fact, the gospel had made a strong impact upon the country. This is seen from references by Tertullian, in the very beginning of the third century, and by Origen about forty-five years later, as well as from the fact that British representatives attended the Councils of Arles (314), Sardica (343), and Ariminum (359). The Anglo-Saxon invaders who began to come across from Germany in 449 were still pagan and destroyed Christianity in eastern England and south-east Scotland. In the west the inhabitants remained Christian and there the Celtic Church developed in association with Ireland and Scotland.

In 597 Augustin and forty followers landed at Ebbsfleet in the isle of Thanet. It was the same year in which St. Columba died in Iona after leading a life of vigorous evangelism in Scotland as well as in his native Ireland. Ethelbert, King of Kent, whose wife, Bertha, was a Christian princess from Paris, made generous provision for the Roman missionaries, but asked for time to study the new faith before accepting it. Within about nine months he and ten thousand of his people professed conversion. Augustin established his headquarters in Canterbury in the church of St. Martin. There grew up the great cathedral which has been so closely bound up with the religious life of England. In 604 Mellitus founded the church of St. Paul's and became the first Bishop of London. Justus became Bishop of Rochester about the same time.

The efforts of Augustin to bring the leaders of the Celtic Church into the Roman communion which he represented completely failed, for they clung passionately to their independence. He died in 604, having barely succeeded in extending the Roman Church beyond Kent. His importance lies in having established Canterbury Cathedral, the influence of which spread later throughout all the land.

Paulinus went from Canterbury to the kingdom of Northumbria in 625 and King Edwin and members of his court were converted. But after a few years the work was entirely destroyed when the pagan king of Mercia killed Edwin, and Paulinus had to flee. The next attempt to bring about the conversion of Northumbria was to come from the Celtic Church of Iona in 635, and this move would scarcely be to the liking of Paulinus because of the differences between their respective communions.

Ever since the arrival of Patrick in Ireland in 432 the gospel had flourished in that land. There is no evidence that he recognized in any way the authority of the See of Rome. In Scotland, the first historical missionary figure is Ninian who built his church and monastery at Whithorn on the Solway Firth in 397 and carried the gospel to the Picts, influencing even the far north. There followed a long succession of saints and preachers. All these have been overshadowed, historically, by St. Columba who came from Ireland to Iona in 563. He was a great statesman, abbot, and evangelist. In 635, Aidan and his friends went from Iona to Lindisfarne, the little island off the coast of Northumberland. Within thirty years they had not only evangelized Northumbria (from the Forth to the Humber) but had reached south almost to the Thames. Rarely has a finer piece of missionary work been done, and yet it has seldom been adequately acknowledged.

From Bangor, in northern Ireland, missionaries were sent out far and near. One of the greatest of these was the zealous and fearless Columbanus who went to Burgundy about twenty years after Columba went to Iona. He founded the famous monasteries of Luxeuil, Annegray, and Fontaine in the region of the Vosges. He had differences from time to time with Pope Gregory I whom he treated with respect, but whose primacy he repudiated.

To this day, in the Vosges, on the Rhine, in Italy, and in distant Hungary there are many monuments which testify to the intrepid work of the Celtic missionaries. For three centuries they were incomparable in learning, piety and missionary activity, and for a time it looked as if they would evangelize all Europe.

In Wales and Cornwall, as well as in Britanny, the Celtic Church also played a great part. At the Synod of Whitby in 664 where representatives of the Roman and Celtic communions discussed their differences, King Oswy of Northumbria was won over to the side of the Church of Rome. From then onwards the influence of the Celtic Church gradually waned throughout Britain but many traces of its great work remained for centuries.[1]

THE CHANGING FACE OF THE CHURCH

Pope Gregory the Great died in 604 and as his reign marked a great step forward in papal power and in

[1] See J. L. G. Meissner, *The Celtic Church in England*, and J. A. Duke, *The Columban Church*.

the development of the Roman Church, it is convenient to glance at some changes in the Church which thrust themselves upon our attention at the beginning of the seventh century. The contrast with the first century is almost startling.

1. *Papal claims*

We are at once arrested by the power now exercised by the pope and the tremendous claims he makes for his office. Instead of being a humble pastor, as were the early presbyters who ministered to the flock of God, he is now able to hold his own with kings and beat them at the diplomatic game. His proud claim is that he is supreme over all the churches and all other bishops.

2. *The Lord's Supper*

Although the Communion was still mainly regarded as a memorial of the death of Christ, the idea was growing fast that it was itself a sacrifice. The doctrine of the Real Presence was widely accepted, although there was no very clear understanding as to what this Presence meant. The idea of a corporal presence was vaguely held by some but it was not till 831 that Paschasius Radbertus published a treatise openly advocating the doctrine of Transubstantiation,[1] and it was practically another four hundred years before it was officially formulated and promulgated as a doctrine of the Roman Church at the Lateran Council in 1215.

3. *Purgatory*

This doctrine had gone on gaining ground ever since Augustine had expressed his belief in its probability as a means of purging souls of their sins by fire. In pagan religions the belief in Purgatory was common. It was thought of as a place under the earth where the souls

---

[1] *Transubstantiation* is the Roman Catholic doctrine that the bread and wine in the Eucharist are changed into the very body and blood of Christ on being consecrated by the priest.

of men were purged through suffering severe torments. The doctrine was favoured by Gregory the Great and was widely accepted, but did not become an article of faith in the Roman Church till the Council of Florence in 1439.

4. *Prayer for the dead and prayers to saints*

These, with their concomitants of Indulgences and Masses for the departed, naturally grew up as the belief in Purgatory increased. Saints and martyrs were greatly venerated, and at the anniversary celebrations at their tombs, the impression grew up that prayers were being offered to them, or for them. Thus, in time, prayers to the Saints came to be regarded as normal. Such prayers were officially recognized by the Church at the Second Council of Nicea in 787.

5. *Adoration of Mary*

Since the Council of Ephesus declared in 431 that Mary was *Theotokos*, 'Mother of God', the cult of Mary went on increasing, though not without great opposition. Festivals (such as that of the Annunciation on March 25) were held in her honour, and then came her worship. By the end of the sixth century, adoration was widely offered her and prayers were addressed to her. Already there was much superstition as to her intervention on behalf of her votaries. The term 'Mother of God' suggests borrowing from paganism, where we find such a conception in expressions used with regard to Demeter, Cybele, and others.[1]

6. *Auricular Confession*

From an early period confession of sin was essential for restoration to church standing after a grievous fall.

---

[1] The full cult of Mary has taken a long time to develop. Thus the doctrine that Mary was born sinless—the Immaculate Conception—was promulgated only in 1854 after centuries of fiery debate especially between the Franciscans and the Dominicans, while the doctrine of the Assumption was not promulgated until the middle of the twentieth century.

At first it was made publicly in church. But since this seemed to foment scandals, it tended, from the days of Leo I (440-461), to become a private Confession before a priest. At that time Confession was permitted but was not compulsory. According to Fleury, a Roman Catholic historian, 'the first time it was commanded' was in 763 by a bishop of Metz.[1]

Strangely enough, the Celtic missionaries on the continent were largely instrumental in popularizing Confession. They had found moral life so low among the Franks that they encouraged men to come privately to confess their sins and receive instruction.

7. Places of worship

With increase of wealth among Christians, and the favour shown to them by the great, their meeting-places became more and more ornate. Examples are the Church of St. Sophia in Constantinople, and the 'seven churches' of Rome in the time of Gregory I. Against the dangers of this sumptuousness Jerome and Chrysostom had given solemn warning about two hundred years earlier, the former declaring that 'that alone is the true temple which is adorned with the indwelling of a true, a holy life'.

By 814 the worship of images in churches had become such a scandal that the emperor Michael wrote in alarm to Louis the Pious, the son of Charlemagne. Long before this the Muslims had begun to taunt the Christians with being idolators because of their image-worship.

8. The priesthood

As sacerdotalism increased, the altar, which formerly had no place in the Christian Church, became of greater and greater importance. This led to drastic alterations which extended even to the achitectural design of churches. The priesthood of all believers was

---

[1] C. A. Fleury, *Ecclesiastical History*, ix, pp. 425–6.

well-nigh forgotten. The priest was now regarded as of a different order from the laity and as having a special grace and divine authority by reason of his ordination. He became indispensable in the Christian's approach to God. He handled divine mysteries and his work was regarded as a species of magic, like the work of the heathen priests. The altar at which he officiated, and upon which he offered again the sacrifice of the body and blood of Christ, came to be regarded as the most sacred place in the building and was railed off from the nave of the church. Thus there grew up a priestly caste separated from the people.

In keeping with this sacerdotalism, vestments which seem to have been first introduced in the reign of Constantine, had come to be regarded as an essential part of the priest's equipment by the end of the sixth century. Both Theodoret and the ecclesiastical historian Socrates tell us that, by the end of the fourth century, bishops were discussing the propriety of different colours for their robes. When Mass came to be celebrated the custom grew up of using special clothes known as Mass vestments, some for High Mass and some for Low. For centuries prior to this the clergy had worn no distinctive clerical dress.

9. *Incense*

The burning of incense was used at first only for the fumigation of Christian buildings. It had no connection with worship for four centuries. As late as the reign of Theodosius I (378-395) enactments ordered the confiscation of houses where it had been used. Both Tertullian and Lactantius (325) refer to the burning of incense as 'pagan', and not practised by Christians.

CHAPTER VII

THE RECORD OF MONASTICISM

THE monastic system, which became so important in the Middle Ages, arose from an unnatural asceticism which was manifesting itself even in the days of St. Paul and which was condemned by him.[1] It was present in the East long before the Christian era, and was strongly developed within Buddhism.

Christian asceticism took its rise from St. Anthony who was born in Egypt in 251 A.D. He forsook wealth and social position, and retired to mountain-caves in order to dedicate himself to lonely contemplation. Later he gathered round him a small group of disciples which he organized into a community in the desert. Members of such communities were known as 'cenobites', meaning 'having life in common', a more accurate term than 'monk' which really means 'a solitary'.

The first great organizer of monastic communities was Pachomius (292-346), who established a monastery at Tabanessi on an island in the Nile in Upper Egypt. When Athanasius visited this community soon after its foundation he was welcomed by 3,000 monks chanting hymns and litanies. This shows the sudden popularity of the movement. By the end of the century very many similar communities had been established in Egypt and the movement had begun to spread elsewhere.

In the West, Monasticism grew up more slowly, in

Cf. [1] Col. ii. 23; 1 Tim. iv. 1-3.

spite of the vigorous support of Athanasius, Jerome, Ambrose and Augustine. One of the very earliest and best leaders in the West was St. Martin of Tours, in Gaul, in the fourth century. Even before the system was practised in Italy he had introduced it to Gaul directly from the East. He greatly influenced St. Ninian who, in 397, established his church and monastery at Whithorn, on the Solway Firth, and took Martin's work as his model. This had powerful effects, not only upon Scotland but upon Ireland as well (Northern Ireland being near Whithorn), and was one of the decisive factors in making the Celtic Church so intensely monastic.

We note briefly the following monastic movements:

1. *The Benedictine Order,* founded by Benedict of Nursia at Mount Cassino in Italy in 529. The discipline was very strict and the Order became immensely popular and very rich. With prosperity and success came degeneracy and abuses.

2. *The Cluniac Movement,* started by Bernon in 910 at Cluny in France to counteract the corruption and lack of zeal which had manifested itself in the Benedictine Order. It stood for the freedom of the Church from all secular interference by princes or patrons, and the free election of bishops and abbots by the chapter or the monks. It also stood out fanatically for clerical celibacy. The influence of Cluny spread far and wide because of its exacting discipline.

3. *The Cistercians,* founded at Citeaux in Burgundy by monks who wanted to keep the original Benedictine rules in their strictness and purity. They aimed at plain, simple living. Bernard founded the famous monastery of Clairvaux in 1115 in a wild and remote valley. His influence was immense and stories regarding the force of his eloquence became legendary. He was, however, very intolerant. The Cistercian Order grew to include 700 monastic houses. The Church has

greatly treasured several of Bernard's hymns such as 'Jesu, the very thought of Thee'.

4. *The Mendicant Orders: the Franciscans and Dominicans*. The members of these Orders were recruited from humble life and their democratic spirit made a wide appeal. They soon completely eclipsed the older Orders, a fact which caused grave jealousies. The founder of the *Franciscans* was the saintly Francis of Assisi in Italy. Their aim was to live a life of poverty in imitation of our Lord. They came to have a dominant position in the Church, counting among their great men Bonaventura, Duns Scotus, and William of Occam. In time they set aside the ideals of St. Francis as to poverty, and entered the same vicious circle as other Orders with regard to wealth and worldliness.

The Dominican Order was founded in 1215 by Dominic, a Spanish nobleman, at the time of the bloody campaign against the Albigenses.[1] Dominic insisted on a simple and austere life to impress the common man, an aim in which he succeeded. The Pope committed to the Dominicans the iniquitous engine of the Inquisition which was to bathe so many lands in blood. It was first established by a Council at Toulouse in 1229 and was supposed to be operated by the bishops.[2]

At their best, the monasteries of the various Orders did a great work in forwarding agriculture, providing schools of learning, caring for the poor, and giving hospitality to the sick and needy. After the founder had died, however, and the first enthusiasm had waned with the growth of wealth and power, it generally happened that they fell into spiritual decadence and in time moved far from their early ideals.

5. *The Military Orders*. These were (i) the Knights of St. John of Jerusalem (founded 1048), (ii) the Knights Templars (founded 1119), and (iii) the Teu-

[1] See p. 98.　　　　[2] See p. 98

tonic Knights (founded 1121). They were all composed of soldier-monks. The Orders began in Palestine with the object of caring for and protecting pilgrims. They soon, however, became very militant and made it their chief object to fight the Saracens. They all became very wealthy and influential and spread to various lands.

CHAPTER VIII

FROM GREGORY I TO CHARLEMAGNE

THE RISE OF ISLAM

THE rise of Islam offered a grave challenge to Christianity and profoundly affected the history of the world. Muhammad was born in Mecca, in Arabia, about 570, and at an early age lost his parents. When he grew to manhood, he prayed much in the solitudes of the desert, fell into trances, and claimed that he heard voices. He had met Jews and heretical Christians who had only apocryphal Gospels. While they gave him the idea that there was but one God, he was not at all impressed by their lives, and this may have prevented him from becoming a Christian. He resolved to replace the degraded polytheism of Arabia by the one, true religion of Allah whose prophet he claimed to be.

Owing to the intense opposition to his preaching, he had to flee from Mecca in 622 and went with some two hundred of his followers to Medina. This 'Hegira' (or 'Hijra'), as his flight was called, was the turning point in his career and from it the Muslim era is dated. Nine years later, after a somewhat chequered career, he re-entered Mecca in triumph, and by the time of his death in 632 he had won over all Arabia.

In the Koran, which Muhammad began writing when he was about forty and which became the sacred book of the Muslims, he recorded what purported to be divine revelations made to him by the angel Gabriel. His character was full of contradictions. He could be friendly and generous, resolute and shrewd; but he could also be fierce and cruel to his enemies, and he was undeniably sensual. Only ninety years after his flight from Mecca in 622, his religion, called by its votaries 'Islam', stretched all the way from India to the Atlantic. Soon it penetrated into Central Asia and China, and later stretched through all southern Asia to Malaya.

Our imagination reels before the magnitude of the disasters which overtook the Church through the Muslim conquests. In the great patriarchates of Antioch, Jerusalem and Alexandria, which extended over vast areas, only remnants of the Christian Church remained. Thus, in Syria alone, 10,000 churches were destroyed or became mosques. The Church of North Africa, with its memories of Tertullian, Cyprian and Augustine, was practically obliterated. Only small Christian communities survived here and there. This destruction of the ancient and illustrious Church east and south of the Mediterranean was nothing less than 'a removing of the candlestick out of its place' (Rev. ii. 5).

After conquering Spain, the Muslim armies pushed across the Pyrenees in 732, and reached the heart of France. All Europe seemed open to them. Then Charles Martel, who was Mayor to the Palace of the Frankish King, marshalled the Christian forces and inflicted a crushing defeat on the invading armies at Tours. It was one of the most important battles in history. As a result of it Europe remained Christian and the Muslim forces were driven back thoroughly defeated.

THE CONVERSION OF THE GERMANIC TRIBES

At the very time when such terrible calamities were falling upon so many of the ancient centres of Church life, the faith was being carried to the Germanic tribes in the neighbourhood of the Rhine. In this work missionaries from Britain played a remarkable part. The great work done by Columbanus[1] was energetically extended by crowds of zealous monks from the Celtic Church in Britain who flocked to evangelize the continent, especially after the Synod of Whitby[2] in 664 when the Roman Church began little by little to absorb their own church at home, and they sought an independent field abroad.

Two great Englishmen did a vast work in building up the Roman Church among the Germanic tribes. The first was *Willibrord,* a native of York, who went as a missionary to Frisia in 690. At first he met considerable opposition from the pagan inhabitants. In spite of this, however, he made very many converts and lived to see the whole region of Frankish Frisia professing Christianity. In 695 he became Archbishop of Utrecht.

Boniface (or Winfrith), another English monk, is often called 'the Apostle of Germany'. A native of Crediton in Devon, he was an able scholar and a born administrator who proved himself invaluable to the Roman Church in founding dioceses, and in building churches and monasteries. His activities in Thuringia, Bavaria and Hesse were conspicuously successful. In 732 he was made an Archbishop, which further increased his influence. He was most subservient to the pope, to whom he swore complete obedience, and as papal legate he himself enjoyed vast prestige. In certain districts he reaped where the Celtic Church had sown and brought their churches and monasteries under the Roman See. He died as a martyr in North Frisia in 753.

In Saxony the way in which, towards the end of the eighth century, the freedom-loving Saxons were compelled by the sword to profess Christianity, is a blot on the name of Charlemagne, who nevertheless had the hearty support of the pope in the action he took. Again

[1] See p. 68.   [2] See p. 68.

and again the Saxons had revolted and wasted the Frankish countryside, slaying priests and burning monasteries. They hated Christianity because it came to them from their enemies, the Franks. As a punishment Charlemagne had 4,500 Saxons beheaded in one day. When, after thirty years of constant fighting (772-803), peace was established, missionaries were sent among them and Germany became, at least nominally, Christian as far as the Elbe. These missionaries found a better way of spreading the gospel than Charlemagne's plan for 'converting the Saxons by the Word and the sword', and soon this valorous people was brought to know Christ.

THE FRANKISH RULERS AND THE HOLY ROMAN EMPIRE

In the eighth century an alliance took place between the Papacy and the Frankish rulers which was to have far-reaching effects for the Church and the world in general. The pope found the support of the powerful Frankish kings, Pepin and Charlemagne, essential because of Lombard hostility and the presence of enemies even in the city of Rome itself. The Frankish kings, for their part, valued the moral support of the Papacy when taking over the throne from the Merovingian line. Hence Pepin was ostentatiously crowned by the papal legate in 752. The pope received from Pepin the lands taken from the exarchate of Ravenna, and known thereafter as 'the patrimony of St. Peter'. This was the beginning of the 'temporal sovereignty' of the popes which was to embroil them in many quarrels. Charlemagne not only saved the pontiff from the Lombards, who were enemies of the Roman See, but in 799 he delivered him from the wrath of the Roman populace who had accused the pope of glaring faults.

On Christmas Day 800, in St. Peter's Church, the pope suddenly advanced and crowned Charlemagne as emperor of the Holy Roman Empire of the West.

He professed to be much surprised, but the indications are that it was all carefully planned beforehand. It was an epoch-making event which affected Europe and the Church for centuries. In the formation of this new Empire there was present the idea of one State and one Church with emperor and pope working hand-in-hand for the glory of God and the welfare of men. In the days of Charlemagne the alliance worked well, but he was always careful to maintain his position as emperor over the pope as well as over everyone else.

The popes claimed that by crowning Charlemagne they had transferred to him the rights of the Eastern emperor, and revived the glories of the ancient Roman Empire. The claim was vigorously resisted on the ground that the crowning was only an acknowledgment of monarchical power which was as effective before the coronation as after, and depended in no way on the See of Rome. The Roman pontiff, however, continued to press his claims for many centuries. It was a sore question and productive of much strife and bitterness. Henceforth the pontiff is found intervening in all kinds of affairs throughout the whole of Christian Europe. With a quiet assurance he assumed that he must be obeyed on the ground of his being the successor of St. Peter. The famous 'capitularies', or laws, of Charlemagne had to do with the Church as much as with secular affairs. He significantly regulated the lives of all the clergy, forbidding them to have wives or concubines, to frequent taverns, or go out hunting, or occupy themselves with worldly business. He also ordained that bishops and abbots should set up their own schools, and wished every parish priest to do the same. This, however, proved difficult to put into effect, but Charlemagne's insistence on the value of learning had a profound influence throughout the Empire and prepared the way for the great scholastic movement of the Middle Ages.

THE WORSHIP OF IMAGES

Gregory the Great, at the beginning of the seventh century, had allowed the use of pictures and images in churches, but insisted that they must not be worshipped. During the eighth century the question sprang into renewed prominence. Prayers were by now addressed to them and they were surrounded by an atmosphere of ignorant superstition, so much so that the Muslims taunted the Christians with being idolaters. It was a sad commentary on the argument of those who had introduced the images because of their beauty and for the instruction of the illiterate.

In 726, the Eastern Emperor, Leo III, interfered to remedy the abuses in his dominion, asking merely that the images and pictures be placed so high that worshippers could not kiss them. The Patriarch of Constantinople and his supporters were furious and before long insurrections broke out there and in Greece and Syria. The emperor and his Council then ordered the complete removal of all images. A bitter fight ensued. Both sides fought on an unspiritual plane. Leo's cause was injured because of the brutality with which his orders were executed. Pope Gregory III denounced the emperor and strongly advocated the use of images. This great controversy is known as the 'iconoclastic' dispute, a word which signifies the breaking of images.

In 754 the emperor Constantine V called a great synod which met at Constantinople. It prohibited image-worship as 'contrary to Scripture' a pagan and anti-Christian practice which led Christians into temptation.[1] The question was a serious one for the Church, since images had become objects of idolatry and incense was burnt before them. Unfortunately, the appeal on both sides of the dispute was to force, violence and abuse throughout the Christian world.

Through the influence of the Empress-Mother,

[1] S. G. Green, *Handbook of Church History*, p. 393.

Irene, the widow of Leo IV who succeeded Constantine V as emperor, the Second Council of Nicea in 787 completely reversed the policy of Leo III, the Isaurian, and decided that images of Christ, the Virgin, saints, and angels could be set up. The Council recommended 'the offering to the images of salutation and honorific worship', and the giving of 'offerings of incense and lights in their honour'—a retrograde policy.

Nevertheless, in the West, in spite of the pope's strong support for the use of images, Charlemagne and the Frankish clergy remained resolutely opposed to them, and emphatically pronounced against them at the Council of Frankfort in 794. Charlemagne in his *Carolingian Books* declared: 'God alone is to be worshipped and adored. Saints are only to be reverenced. Images are by no means to be worshipped.'

CHAPTER IX

DISORDER AND INTRIGUE

THE FALSE DECRETALS

OF all the strange chapters in church history none is more amazing than the story of the forged Decretals and the supposed Donation of Constantine. *Decretals* is a general term for papal decrees, judicial decisions, mandates, edicts and similar official pronouncements. The fabricated decretals were put in circulation about 850 by some unscrupulous Frankish ecclesiastic, and the collection was ascribed to the renowned Isidore of Seville, a great prelate and writer of the early seventh century. The real decretals of the popes went back only to Siricius (384-398), but in this collection there were now embodied letters, decisions and laws of the Bishop of Rome supposedly going back to the first century, together with various other spurious ecclesiastical and State documents. The forger was a most skilful worker, and obviously well educated.

The aim was to support the stupendous claims then being made by the pope for dominance in Church and State, and at the same time to bolster up the unscriptural pretensions of the clergy. On such a false foundation the mighty power of the Roman Church was very largely built up. Since the Renaissance in the fifteenth century, scholars have realized that the documents were spurious; but this realization did not affect in the slightest degree the imposing edifice which was erected on these false foundations.

THE DONATION OF CONSTANTINE

This was another forged document in which it was alleged that, when Constantine was baptized by Pope Sylvester in 324, he presented him with the Lateran Palace and all the insignia of the Western Empire, with the whole of Italy, and other provinces of the Roman Empire. The falsity of this appears at once, for Constantine was not baptized by Sylvester at all, but by Eusebius of Nicomedia, an Arian bishop, and in 337, not 324. The aim of the forgery was to antedate by about five hundred years the pope's temporal power which, as we have seen, was actually granted by Pepin and Charlemagne. Neither Constantine nor any of his successors ever dreamt of giving away to the Bishop of Rome their temporal power in the West. It is not necessary to believe that any pope actually took part in the production of these forgeries; but they acted upon them, perhaps innocently, in later generations, and without question this strengthened their claims to almost limitless authority. The first to base his claims upon these false documents was Pope Nicholas I (858-867). He proudly proclaimed, 'that which the pope has decided is to be observed by all,' and he showed his authority by compelling Hincmar, the powerful Archbishop of Rheims, to reinstate Rothad, the Bishop of Soissons, whom he had deposed. He also obliged the emperor Lothair II to take back his queen whom he had divorced, and, in spite of many threats, he deposed two archbishops who had aided the monarch in his evil designs.

DISORDER IN THE CHURCH

Nicholas succeeded against Hincmar and Lothair because they were morally in the wrong. His two successors, Pope Hadrian II (867-872), and John VIII (872-882) claimed the right to interfere in political disputes and even to dispose of the imperial crown; but they fared badly, the latter coming to a violent end in 882. Then ensued a period of incredible disorder when the popes were constantly embroiled in the political quarrels of the age and many of them perished ignominiously. The descendants of Charlemagne had fallen into disrepute because of their incapacity and debauchery. The last emperor of the Carolingian house was Charles the Fat, who was deposed in 887. Thus ended the great Empire founded by Charlemagne.

In this time of misgovernment, the Norse pirates threatened to submerge Europe once more in barbarism. They attacked the coasts of Germany and France destroying great seaports, and they carried fire and sword right along the Rhine valley. They accepted Christianity at last and settled down in Normandy, from which they conquered England in 1066. The Muslim armies crossed over from Africa in the ninth century and took possession of Sicily and Southern Italy, bringing havoc in their train, while the Hungarian Magyars were threatening Europe from the east. All this had a very evil effect on both civil and religious life. Schaff says: 'Within the limits of nominal Christendom, the kings and nobles quarrelled among themselves, oppressed the people, and distributed bishoprics and abbeys among their favourites, or pocketed the income. The metropolitans oppressed the bishops, the bishops the priests, and the priests the laity. Bands of robbers roamed over the country and defied punishment.'[1]

After the deposition of Charles the Fat in 887, the Italian nobles became very powerful and fought one another for pre-eminence. The Church suffered severely in the prevailing disorder. According to Schaff, the papacy 'became the prey of avarice, violence and intrigue, a veritable synagogue of Satan. Pope followed pope in rapid succession, and most of them ended their career in deposition, prison and

[1] Philip Schaff, *Mediaeval Christianity*, I, p. 282.

murder. The rich and powerful marquises of Tuscany and the Counts of Tusculum acquired control of Rome and the papacy for more than half a century.'[1]

During this time three strong-minded women of high rank, but of very low morals, dominated the papacy. Theodora the elder, and her two daughters, Marozia and Theodora, filled the papal chair with their paramours and illegitimate children. They were beautiful but utterly unscrupulous women, and the vile tale of their immoralities with popes and nobles is shocking to the last degree. The facts have been frankly recognized, and not without indignation, by Roman Catholic historians of high standing, like Baronius and Luitprand.[2] Meanwhile the old idea of a Holy Roman Empire still influenced many hearts. Various attempts were made to revive it but failed. In 960 Pope John XII, one of the worst of the pontiffs, appealed to Otto I, King of Germany, to protect him against Berengar II of Italy. Otto came to the help of the papacy as Pepin and Charlemagne had previously done. The new Empire formed by him was smaller than that of Charlemagne and is often called the Holy Germanic Empire because the Teutonic influence was dominant. When Pope John turned against Otto, the latter retaliated by getting a Synod of St. Peter's Church to depose the pontiff on charges of murder, blasphemy, and gross sensuality. Otto was a strong monarch and, in spite of insurrections, helped to save the papacy morally, but at the loss of its independence.

Early in the eleventh century matters again went from bad to worse with the papacy. At one stage, from 1044 to 1046, there were three very unworthy men each claiming to be pontiff. They were Benedict IX, Sylvester III, and Gregory VI. The emperor Henry III was asked by a Synod in 1046 to nominate future popes

[1] Philip Schaff, *Mediaeval Christianity*, I, p. 283.
[2] See Philip Schaff, *op. cit.* I, pp. 277–292, for an ampler and well-documented account. Also H. H. Milman, *Latin Christianity*, III, pp. 284–316.

and this saved the Church from chaos at that time. Then arose a reforming party at Rome aiming to expand papal power at everyone's expense. Among them was an able and astute young monk, Hildebrand, who earnestly supported the edict promulgated by Nicholas II in 1059 to place the election of the pope in the hands of the college of Cardinals alone, without the intervention of either emperor or Diet. Hildebrand quickly became the adviser and, indeed, the master of successive popes. His methods were brutal, involving the free use of military force.

THE SPREAD OF CHRISTIANITY IN EUROPE (800-1073)

Early in the ninth century, Ansgar carried the gospel to Denmark and Norway, but all Scandinavia did not become Christian till late in the eleventh century. In 846 Rastiz slaughtered his subjects in Moravia until he succeeded in making his domain ostensibly Christian. In 848 fourteen Bohemian princes were baptized, but the people fought stoutly against Christianity because it came to them from German sources. In 860, Boris, King of Bulgaria, followed the dreadful policy of Rastiz and massacred many. In 968 Poland became nominally Christian. The Magyars fell under Christian influences from 973 onwards through the work of Piligrim. The Russians received the gospel from Constantinople in 988, through emissaries of the Greek Orthodox Church, sent at the request of King Vladimir. Russia became one of the great bulwarks of the Greek Orthodox Church and made up somewhat for the terrible losses sustained elsewhere through the conquests of Islam.

By the end of the thirteenth century at least nominal Christianity covered all Europe except Finland and Lapland.

CHAPTER X

GREGORY VII TO BONIFACE VIII
(1073-1294)

THE PAPACY AT ITS HEIGHT

WHEN Hildebrand became pope in 1073, taking the name of Gregory VII, he carried through a revolution in the position of the Church. He held that, as vicar of Christ and representative of Peter, he could give or take away 'empires, kingdoms, duchies, marquisates, and the possessions of all men'. Everyone on earth, from the emperor down to the humblest peasant, must acknowledge him.

He began his campaign by a scathing attack on the theory which had allowed some priests to marry. Henceforth the priests of the Roman Church were a class apart, cut off from the most sacred and elevating experiences of family life. His next attack was on simony. There was need for action here, for unscrupulous princes and others not infrequently sold sacred offices to the highest bidder irrespective of spiritual qualifications. Hildebrand's greatest fight, however, was over the question of *lay investiture*. Under feudal law a vassal had to do homage to his lord on taking possession of lands. He was then presented with a symbol in recognition of his legal rights. The same applied when certain offices were taken up. This ceremony was called *investiture*. As the great churchmen held lands and domains, they had to be invested like others. Hildebrand, following the Cluniac teaching, objected strongly to all interference of the secular power in church affairs and held that ecclesiastics should take up office without any sanction from the civil ruler. The secular powers, however, were not without solid grounds for their attitude. In some countries virtually half the property belonged to the Church. To have dispensed with homage and transferred vast territories to the pope would have meant chaos in civil government.

In 1075 Hildebrand boldly prohibited lay investiture and summoned the emperor Henry IV to Rome as if he were a feudal vassal. When Henry refused and persuaded a German Council to depose the pope, the latter placed him under Interdict. The emperor found himself abandoned by all. No one would have any dealings with him, or give him food or shelter, for fear of eternal torments, so great was the terror inspired then by a papal Interdict. Within a year he hurried across the Alps in the depth of winter with his wife and child to make his peace with the pontiff. He went to the palace of Canossa where the pope then was. Barefooted, and dressed as a humble penitent, he was compelled to stand for three days in the courtyard in the snow. On the fourth day the pontiff deigned to receive him. He pled for clemency, confessed his fault, and made his humble submission at the feet of the pope, and received absolution. The triumph of the papacy seemed complete.

In the end, however, after a war with his rival, Rudolf of Swabia, Henry emerged triumphant. In spite of powerful support from the army of Robert Guiscard of Sicily, Hildebrand was driven out, and Henry, whose victory was overwhelming, appointed an antipope, Clement III, in his place. In 1085 Hildebrand, the Napoleon of the eleventh century, died in exile at Salerno, declaring: 'I have loved righteousness and hated iniquity, therefore I die in exile.'

Although he ended his life in eclipse, his principles were accepted and cherished by his successors. Men could never forget that even the secular head of the

Holy Roman Empire had had to fall prostrate at the feet of the pontiff. The Hildebrandine party appointed as pope Urban II, a very adroit and skilful leader of men. Like his successor, Paschal II, he encouraged the sons of Henry IV to revolt. His influence grew enormously, especially after he started the Crusades, while that of the anti-pope dwindled away. In 1122, in the Concordat of Worms, an agreement was reached with Henry V on the vexed question of lay investiture. The emperor agreed to substitute the touch of the monarch's sceptre for investiture by ring and crozier, the election to be in his presence but without his interference. Thus ended one of the most difficult questions of the Middle Ages.

By the beginning of the twelfth century, the strong and prosperous cities of Lombardy became republican in outlook. Among their leaders arose Arnold of Brescia (1100-1153), a pupil of the famous Abelard. He urged a return to the simplicity of life of New Testament times, and manifested some of the spirit of the Reformation. One of his great opponents was Bernard of Clairvaux. In 1143 he was received with wild enthusiasm in Rome where a Republic had been proclaimed. In the fighting which ensued, one pope was slain, and the next had to flee to France.

The young emperor, Frederick Barbarossa, marched into Italy and overcame temporarily the Lombard League. To ingratiate himself with the pope he handed over the fearless Arnold of Brescia who was put to death.

The friendship of Frederick with the pope was, however, short-lived. When, in 1176 at Legnano, Frederick was thoroughly beaten by the Lombard cities, the outcome was astonishing. On July 24, 1177, outside St. Mark's Church in Venice, the great Frederick Barbarossa spread his cloak upon the pavement, knelt before Pope Alexander and kissed his feet. Then he behaved like a menial, holding the pope's stirrup and leading his horse by the bridle along the street. It was an even greater triumph for Pope Alexander than was Canossa for Hildebrand a century earlier.

THE CRUSADES (1095-1270)

The idea of a Crusade, actively espoused by Hildebrand, was carried out by his successors. The fanaticism of the rough Turkish Muslims who captured Jerusalem from the Arabs had become a menace to Christendom, and pilgrims were being seriously interfered with. Pope Urban II threw all his strength into preparing for the First Crusade. He was quick to see the moral prestige which would accrue to himself and the papal system through his leadership of the movement. He was not mistaken. He deeply moved his audiences by his lurid descriptions of Saracen barbarities against pilgrims. To persuade the people to take part, many kinds of inducements were held out—absolution from all kinds of sin; eternal blessedness for the fallen; miracles to help; cancellation of debts; pardon for criminals, and it is safe to say that the Crusades did more to popularize Indulgences than any other single influence.

Peter the Hermit, an uncouth and unkempt preacher, worked up the multitudes into a frenzy of enthusiasm. It was soon regarded as a disgrace not to join the Crusade. Many thousands of men, women and children, in various unofficial expeditions, set out in 1096 without any preparation, expecting to be miraculously provided for. Of 275,000 who joined these groups all either perished of cold or disease, or were scattered. Peter himself fled at the first sign of danger.

The first official Crusade, with 300,000 men,[1] set out in August 1096, going via Constantinople. Tens of thousands perished in the cold uplands of Asia Minor. Rivalries and jealousies also sadly weakened the expedition, but their bravery was unbounded. They

---

[1] Estimates vary from 150,000 to 600,000.

reached Jerusalem in 1099. Of those who left Europe only one tenth completed the journey. Legend told for centuries of the miracles supposed to have taken place in the siege. It is a strange reflection on the spirit of the Crusade that when they entered the Holy City, their first action was to massacre the Saracens.

This was the only one of the eight Crusades which can really claim to have achieved what it set out to do. The Second Crusade was an unmitigated failure, although sponsored by the most powerful men in Europe. It was organized when the Turks captured Edessa from the Christians in 1144. The recapture of Jerusalem in 1187 by Saladin, the Saracen leader, was a sore blow to Christian sentiment and led to the Third Crusade. The emperor Frederick Barbarossa, Philip of France, and Richard Coeur de Lion of England, all set out for Palestine with strong armies. Barbarossa was drowned while crossing the River Selef in Seleucia. Philip and Richard, in spite of unsurpassable heroism, virtually failed in their mission. The Fourth and Sixth Crusades were successful in a way, but their achievements were not fully recognized by the pope. The Fifth, Seventh, and Eighth were all lamentable failures. Nearly all Europe, apart from the pope, heaved a sigh of relief when in 1270 the Crusades were abandoned.

Men had entered the Crusades with very mixed motives. The immorality, pillage and massacre which so often disgraced the movement show that in spite of great zeal in pursuance of an ideal, no true spiritual power had taken possession of them. The effects were mainly political and social rather than religious.

POPE INNOCENT III

In the time of Pope Innocent III (1198-1216), the papacy reached the height of its power. In policy he followed Hildebrand but he was more successful in carrying it out. Circumstances favoured him. The humiliation of Henry IV at Canossa and of Barbarossa at Venice had led the people to believe that the pope was all-powerful and that every ruler was under his authority. Moreover, the enthusiasm engendered by the Crusades had greatly strengthened papal prestige. The success of Innocent III was dramatic. Both King John of England and the powerful Philip of France were humiliated and brought to their knees. It is not too much to say that Pope Innocent's political power extended in one way or another over almost all Christian lands. In Italy itself he moulded everything to his will, ruling most effectively over the papal dominions. The pontiff had, once more, a real temporal power.

In the more spiritual domain, he instituted the Fourth Crusade, which, however, violated all his orders. He launched a full scale war against what he regarded as heresy, and his persecution of the Albigenses,[1] a heroic sect in southern France, will always stand out as a crying scandal. His magnificence reached its culminating point in the splendour of the Lateran Council in 1215, one of the greatest Ecumenical Councils of all time.

POPE BONIFACE VIII

The mighty power of the papacy, which was brought to its height by Innocent III, continued in unabated strength until the days of Boniface VIII (1294-1303) when it began to decline. Boniface insisted most strongly that all temporal rulers were subject to him; and in his bull 'Unam Sanctam' he wrote 'we declare, state, define and pronounce that for every human creature to be subject to the Roman pope is altogether necessary for salvation'. Further than this the claims of the papacy could not go. The very arrogance of the papal claims, however, irritated many rulers and provoked violent reactions. This is clearly demonstrated in the conflicts waged by Edward I of England and

[1] See also p. 98.

Philip the Fair of France against the pope. Finally, Philip sent a servant, Nogaret, to Italy, and Boniface was arrested at Anagni. So roughly was he treated, that he died within a month. This was symptomatic of a great change in the attitude of nations towards the papacy. Not only had the pride and power of the popes sown the seeds of spiritual decay, but the growing nationalist spirit in the various countries heralded the opening of an era of hostility to the papal claims. It was not so easy to manage a number of national rulers as it had been to control a single emperor.

THE AVIGNON POPES

The next step in the weakening of the papacy was the removal of the popes to Avignon, on the Rhone. Pope Clement V (1305-1313) was so much under the power of Philip of France that he could not face the indignation of the Italian people. He resided first at Bordeaux and then Poitiers, but in 1309 removed to Avignon. The popes resided outside Italy for over seventy years, a period which some ardent Roman Catholics have designated as 'the Babylonish Captivity' of the Church, for it was a time of miserable servitude to the French monarchy. The situation in Rome in the long absence of the popes became dangerous for the Church politically and religiously. Great efforts were made by Roman citizens and other influential people to get the pope back and in 1377 Gregory XI returned from the long exile.

THE GREAT SCHISM (1378-1417)

Scarcely had one scandal ended when a greater began. On the death of Pope Gregory in 1378, Urban VI, an Italian, was elected. The French cardinals elected a fellow countryman, Clement VII, who returned to Avignon. Some nations supported the pope at Avignon, some the pope at Rome. So serious was this schism that the power of Rome was never the same again. Catholics had believed that their salvation de-pended on acknowledging the successor of Peter. Here were two popes for nearly forty years, each anathema-tizing the other, and each claiming to be the only true occupant of Peter's chair. No wonder the Catholic world was perplexed.

CHAPTER XI

RISING OPPOSITION TO THE CATHOLIC CHURCH

ABOUT the middle of the seventh century there had appeared a Christian sect, called the Paulicians, in the region of the Euphrates. They spread to Armenia, Asia Minor, and Thrace. Somewhat akin to them were the Bogomils (a term meaning 'Friends of God') in Bulgaria and Bosnia, in the tenth century. Later still, under the name of Cathari (or, *The Pure*), various groups of ascetic-minded Christians, characterized by a marked reverence for the Scriptures, spread from the Balkans westwards. From the end of the twelfth century the Beghards, a praying people, flourished in the Netherlands and along the Rhine. In the twelfth and thirteenth centuries the Albigenses became very numerous in southern France, and the Waldenses in northern Italy.

In all these sects, and in others besides, we find a strong testimony being borne against the errors prevailing in the Catholic Church. They attracted a numerous following of passionately earnest men. Their doctrines were not identical, and, in some cases at least, heresy existed among them. The favourite accusation of the Catholic Church was that they were Manichaeans, that is that they followed the ascetic practices and the doctrines of Mani who tried to reconcile Christianity with Zoroastrianism, the ancient faith of Persia, which believed in an eternal dualism of light and darkness. But whatever else these numerous sects stood for, they represented a common trend to organize life and worship independently of the Roman Catholic clergy, and on the basis of the Bible in the vernacular. They pled for a simple, devout life. Not all the popes condemned them.

The best known were the Albigenses. They regarded the clergy of their time as corrupt, and counted their rites as worthless because they were not men of God. Their persecution began under the Bishop of Citeaux and Simon de Montfort. It lasted for twenty years and in the end almost exterminated them. Since the bishops, in dealing with opposition of this kind, had put little heart into their use of the Inquisition,[1] in 1231 Pope Gregory IX put this engine of iniquity into the hands of the Dominican Order, giving its leaders vast powers to coerce bishops and nobles whose help they wanted in their nefarious work. They were only too successful. Archbishop R. C. Trench says: 'The machinery, so wonderful in its wickedness and its craft, did not fail in its object. . . . By the middle of the fourteenth century there were probably few Albigenses more.'[2] It is certain that, although outwardly suppressed, the spirit of these persecuted sects continued to live in the hearts of the people till the Reformation. Much historical research is still called for in order to bring out the true story and the theological position of those numerous bodies. There are complicated questions involved and in the past historians have depended too much on the statements of the enemies of the dissenting groups for their assessment of their doctrine and morals.

OPPOSITION FROM WITHIN THE CATHOLIC CHURCH

We look now at some of those who were not outside the Catholic Church, but contended against its policy and practice from within. One of the most remarkable was Marsilius of Padua (1270-1342), a physician by pro-

---

[1] Cf. p. 75.
[2] R. C. Trench, *Mediaeval Church History*, p. 219.

fession. In his *Defensor Pacis,* written in Paris in 1324, he maintained that the supreme standard is the Bible. The supreme authority is a General Council made up of representative clergy and laymen. The clergy are equal, he declares, and such offices as those of popes and bishops are of human origin. The clergy should be appointed by the civil authorities, on behalf of the people. Excommunication by a priest is nothing unless it coincides with the judgment of God. Such declarations seem remarkable for that epoch, but they were merely a development of ideas current for some time amongst both papalist and anti-papalist thinkers.

A far greater man, an Englishman, William of Occam (1280-1347), the renowned Nominalist philosopher at the University of Paris, and a leading Franciscan, expressed views not unlike these. Such men represented the strong, rising individualism of the epoch, and the determination not to accept blindly all that emanated from the high ecclesiastical authorities.

JOHN WYCLIF (1320-1384)

John Wyclif was in his day the ablest scholar at Oxford, a University with which he had a life-long connection. Although a priest of the Roman Church to his dying day, he declared that 'the only head of the Church is Christ. The pope, unless he be one of the predestinate who rule in the spirit of the gospel, is the vicar of Antichrist'. 'The power-grasping hierarchy, and the monks and friars, who claim special religious sanctity are without Scriptural warrant.' He rejected Transubstantiation[1] utterly as contrary to both Scripture and reason. He denied the infallibility of the Roman Church in matters of faith, rejected auricular confession, and criticized belief in Purgatory, pilgrimages, worship of saints and veneration of relics, as being all unscriptural. No wonder he has been acclaimed as 'The morning star of the English Reformation'.

[1] Cf. p. 43 and p. 69.

He organized bands of preachers who lived very simply and went throughout the land preaching the Word at a time when the priests seldom preached and the people were left uninstructed. Nor can we exaggerate the importance of the translation of the Vulgate into English made by his followers—the first Bible in our language. Its effects were far-reaching for it brought home the truth to prince and peasant alike.

The reception given by the laity to Wyclif's writings reveals how widespread was the desire for reform of the Church. Hundreds of monks and nuns also welcomed these writings, but there was, naturally enough, much opposition. His enemies would gladly have burnt him, but, in the providence of God, he was protected by the Court, especially by John of Gaunt. The motive was, perhaps, political rather than religious. It expressed their hostility to the pope, then living at Avignon, and a puppet of the French King with whom the English were at enmity.

JOHN HUS (1360-1415)

This man, born a poor peasant, became by sheer ability Rector of Prague University, then the most important university in Europe after Paris and Oxford. He had a genuine experience of conversion, and became a powerful preacher in the Bohemian language, proclaiming the gospel with fiery zeal and rebuking fearlessly the common vices. The clergy turned on him only when he attacked their own covetousness, sloth and luxury. In those days there were close links between the universities of Oxford and Prague, and the teachings of Wyclif made a deep impression on Hus and others in Bohemia. As he was a perfervid patriot the Germans avenged themselves by charging him with heresy. His books were publicly burnt at Prague, and the archbishop tried to stop his preaching.

Eventually Hus was summoned before the Council of Constance. Relying on a safe conduct granted him by Sigismund, the German king and emperor elect, he went. He was thrown into prison and barbarously treated. The emperor gave an order for his release but was terrified into cancelling it by the pope and cardinals. After seven months of cruel suffering Hus was put through a mockery of a trial. His defence was drowned with shouts of 'Recant, Recant!' He declared he would retract nothing unless it was contrary to God's Word. In 1415, after the most shameful degradation by the Council, he was burnt at their request outside Constance by the civil authorities.

It is ironic that Pope John XXIII who, with the Council, was responsible for the death of this righteous man was himself steeped in wickedness. The historian, Margaret Deansley, calls him 'a clerical brigand', and Archbishop R. C. Trench records that, before this same Council of Constance was over, he was compelled to resign 'accused of crimes strange for their multitude and enormity, and not daring to face an investigation'.[1]

---

[1] R. C. Trench, *Mediaeval Church History*, p. 291.

CHAPTER XII

ATTEMPTED REFORMATION
AND THE RENAISSANCE

THE REFORMING COUNCILS

THE development of a new attitude to the papacy is clearly seen in the three Reforming Councils which took place during the years 1409 to 1449. To find a solution of the Great Schism,[1] men like John Gerson, Chancellor of the University of Paris, and Cardinal d'Ailly of the same University, were driven to propose a General Council. They held that such a gathering, representative of the whole body of the Church, was superior to the pope, and could judge him and remove him, and reform the Church. Thus it was that the Council of Pisa (1409) deposed the two rival popes, Gregory XII and Benedict XIII, declaring them to be notorious schismatics, heretics, and perjurers, and elected Pope Alexander V. When, however, the Council proceeded to the work of reformation, they were thwarted by the new pope who wanted no curbing of his powers, and on the earliest opportunity he dissolved the gathering.

The Second Council was held at Constance from 1414 to 1418. It was this gathering which condemned John Hus to death, an act which cost the Roman Church much support. As we have seen[2] it also compelled Pope John XXIII to resign because of his 'detestable and unseemly life and manners', and appointed Cardinal Colonna to succeed him, who took the name Martin V. It also again deposed the rival popes,

[1] See p. 95.   [2] See p. 101.

Gregory XII (who died during the Council) and Benedict XIII (who refused to acknowledge its sentence and maintained his claim to be the lawful pope until his death in 1424). Although the Council had little or no success in effecting any lasting reform it is important since it declared that its authority was derived 'immediately from Christ' and was effective over the pope as well as over other members of the Church. As Bishop W. S. Kerr has pointed out,[1] 'The proceedings at Constance are a full and comprehensive rebuttal of the Vatican Decrees that the pope is placed over the universal Church. . . . The legitimacy of Martin V and all his successors to the present day depends on the lawful authority of the Council over the popes.'

The Third Council met at Basel in 1431 to deal with the Hussite revolt in Bohemia and generally to seek reform of the Church. The pope tried to dissolve it but its members refused to obey his orders, again maintaining that a General Council was superior to the pope. With the passing of the years, however, it lost credit and was finally dissolved by the emperor Frederick III in 1449.

Although these Councils failed to secure even a moderate reform, it was well that they had raised this serious question of the need for it. The disease was more deadly than they knew. Others after them were to tinker with the matter of reform, for everywhere its necessity was realized; but only a Martin Luther could bring it to pass, and that in the only way it could be done—by laying an axe to the roots of the whole papal system.

THE RENAISSANCE

Of all the factors, other than religious ones, which prepared for the Reformation, the great movement

[1] W. S. Kerr, *A Handbook on the Papacy*, p. 261.

called the Renaissance was the chief. It was not a religious movement, but it prepared the way for the Reformers by opening men's minds and breaking the shackles imposed for centuries by the hierarchy. The word Renaissance means 'a rebirth', and is used to designate the revival of Latin and Greek literature and art which took place at the end of the mediaeval period and the beginning of the modern age. A new spirit was abroad—a spirit of adventure, enterprise, geographical discovery and intellectual quickening. Arabic translations of Greek authors, especially Aristotle, had helped to counteract the sad neglect of Greek culture in Europe, in the Middle Ages; and, in the fourteenth century, Dante, Petrarch and Boccaccio had helped to revive interest in the classical writers. The use of the printing press spread knowledge among the masses as never before. The dry and sterile word-spinning of Scholasticism was replaced by the methods of genuine science with its new and precious discoveries, while philosophy, too, was entering on a new era.

When in 1453, Constantinople fell to the Turks, many great scholars fled to the West, bringing not only knowledge, but treasures of Greek literature which had been carefully preserved throughout the years. Several of the popes were most enthusiastic supporters of the New Learning and the Arts, not realizing that the new spirit of independent enquiry would deal a deadly blow to the authoritarian system which the papacy represented.

Nicolas V, the illustrious founder of the Vatican Library, was the first pope to interest himself in the Renaissance. Artists and scholars were greatly helped by him, and he ordered many Greek classics to be translated into Latin. Some of the greatest architects, artists and sculptors the world has ever known flourished during this era. Among them were Donato Bramante, Raphael, Michael Angelo and Leonardo da Vinci. They were employed on the great work of building and decorating St. Peter's at Rome, and the beauty of their work astonishes all visitors.

The devotees of the New Learning were called Humanists. In Holland and Germany they were definitely more Christian in their outlook than in Italy, chiefly because of the excellent influence of the schools of the Brethren of the Common Life which began at Deventer in 1376 and stressed the importance of religion in education. They produced many brilliant men such as Erasmus, Mutianus Rufus, and John Wessel of Groningen, scholars who prepared the way for the Reformation. Little by little the New Learning entered the universities, the schools and the leading social circles. Some of its exponents were cruelly persecuted, for example, the great scholar Reuchlin.

Among outstanding Christian Humanists, we notice the following:

1. *Savonarola* (1452-1498). Although he still accepted the mediaeval theology, he profoundly affected the lives of many scholars in days when the Renaissance had led a great number of them into the sensualism of paganism in his native Italy. His saintliness and earnest preaching profoundly affected the masses, transformed the lives of intellectuals, and caused fashionable women to make 'a bonfire of vanities' in the public square. He aimed at making Florence a theocratic Republic. He was unjustly charged with heresy, and was strangled and burnt in 1498. Thus the Roman Church did to death one of the noblest of her sons and showed that purification of the Roman system was impossible as it was then constituted.

2. *John Colet* (1466-1519). He was one of a group of brilliant Humanists at Oxford and fell under the influence of the ideas spread by Savonarola. He broke away from the methods of Scholasticism, and his lectures on Paul's Epistles caused a sensation, because he made the apostle's message live again. Becoming

Dean of St. Paul's, he preached in 1512 a startling sermon before Convocation in which he declared that the vicious and depraved lives of the clergy were the worst heresy of the times. First reform the bishops, he declared, and it will spread to all and sundry. The laws of the Church would never be enforced until the bishops became new men. He taught his students that the important matter was to keep the Bible and the Apostles' Creed. He believed in no priesthood and denied transubstantiation.

Among his famous students were Erasmus, whom he persuaded to produce his Greek version of the New Testament, and William Tyndale, to whom we owe so much for his English translation of the Bible which cost him his life at the stake.

3. *Desiderius Erasmus* (1467-1536). Born at Rotterdam, he became easily the greatest of the Humanists. For a short time he was professor of Divinity and Greek at Cambridge. His literary labours were incessant. His *Enchiridion, In Praise of Folly* and *Colloquies* abounded in raillery against the Mediaeval Church, its ceremonies, and clergy. His aim was to reform the Church of Rome from within and when, during the Reformation, many were leaving her, he refused to do so. He was scathingly attacked by both Roman Catholics and Protestants and was accused of lack of courage. His Greek edition of the New Testament was invaluable. He wanted to make it understood not only by 'women', but by 'Scots and Irish, and by Turks and Saracens'.

The study of the great classics of Greece and Rome, and the enthusiasm for Greek art, carried men back to pagan ideals, with the result that a great degeneration of morals ensued. On the one hand we have the beautiful works of art which were being produced for St. Peter's and the Vatican, and for churches throughout Italy. On the other hand we find men indulging to excess their love of pleasure and becoming treacherous and perfidious in their dealings with each other. Poison, the dagger and the gun were freely used to secure the aims of the ambitious. It was the period of Caesar and Lucretia Borgia (children of Pope Alexander VI), and they represented 'all the elegance, all the vices, and all the crimes of that epoch', in spite of their being outstanding supporters of the Renaissance movement. The popes themselves were far from being models of correct living. Obviously something more than the New Learning and a love of art, however beautiful, was required to make saints. The greatest gain from the Renaissance was that it broke the shackles which the mediaeval Church had placed upon thought and investigation.

Although many of the greatest Christian Humanists died still members of the Roman Church, it would be impossible to exaggerate their importance as precursors of the Reformation. The effect of Renaissance scholarship in general was to lead men back to the original Greek and Hebrew documents—past the Vulgate and imperfect translations of patristic texts. Thus it was possible, once again, to return to the teachings of the early Church on important matters and to rediscover truths which had long been obscured by incorrect renderings of Scripture.

CHAPTER XIII

THE REFORMATION IN GERMANY

MARTIN LUTHER

THE Humanists, although they had prepared the way, had produced no reformation in the Church. To do this, a man was required of intense spiritual conviction, on fire with zeal for the gospel and possessing, in addition, great ability and courage. Such a man was Martin Luther, the originator and leader of the Reformation in Germany.

Born on November 10, 1483, the son of a poor miner, he knew the struggles and the outlook of the working-classes. Having obtained a free education at Eisenach School, he entered Erfurt University in 1501. There the influence of John Wesel, the Christian Humanist, had left a decided impression. Luther was a brilliant law student, fond of music and philosophy. Suddenly, however, and to the surprise of all his friends, he entered the Convent of the Augustinian Eremites. From boyhood he had had a keen sense of the reality of the spiritual world. His Pelagian[1] teachers now taught him to save himself through prayers, fasting and penance. The Scriptures were withheld from him, but he wearied his superiors with his constant confessions and penance. And still he found no rest. Then, when he was twenty, he discovered a Latin Bible. John Staupitz, his Vicar-General, encouraged him to read it, and pointed him to Christ Jesus who alone takes away sin and gives us fellowship with God. While reading Romans the peace of God came into Luther's

[1] See pp. 57f.

heart. Through studying Augustine's works he came to see even more clearly that men are saved by God through Jesus Christ and not by their own good works, and that this salvation depends on God's grace alone. The monastic life and external observances in religion became of less importance to him. He began carefully to study the Hebrew and Greek Scriptures, especially Paul's Epistles.

Tetzel and the Indulgences

Pope Leo X (1513-1521) needed great sums of money to continue the building of St. Peter's Church, and to gratify his own extravagant tastes. To secure the money, he resolved to extend the sale of Indulgences. Such sales had produced grave abuses in the past and the new drive for money brought matters to a climax. A famous seller of Indulgences, a Dominican monk, named Tetzel, shamefully offered his wares near Wittenberg, declaring that 'no sooner will the money chink in the box, than the soul of the departed will be free' from Purgatory. The spirit of Martin Luther was stirred to the depths. On All Saints' Day, 1517, he nailed his Ninety-five Theses to the church door at Wittenberg where vast crowds congregated. In this famous document it was emphatically laid down, among other things, (a) that an Indulgence can never remit guilt; God has kept that in His own hand; (b) it cannot remit divine punishment for sin; that also is in God's hand alone; (c) it has no efficacy for souls in Purgatory; and (d) the Christian who has true repentance has already received pardon from God, and needs no Indulgence.

Copies were made in German of the Latin Theses and printed off by friends for circulation in tens of thousands all over Germany. The conflict had begun which was to usher in the Reformation.

The issues raised were far greater than even Luther himself knew. The pope thought it was merely 'a squabble of monks', but he soon realized his mistake and summoned Luther to Rome in July 1518. To have gone would have meant certain death, and he therefore refused. Then the pope asked his legate in Germany, Cardinal Cajetan, to deal with the question. On meeting Luther at Augsburg, he objected to statements in the Theses such as that the merits of Christ free the sinner without papal intervention. Luther, however, refused to recant, appealed 'from the pope ill-informed to the pope better-informed', and returned to Wittenberg. Up till now, Luther had accepted the pope's supremacy; but when he began to examine the arguments for it he was filled with indignation to find that the claims were based on the Forged Decretals.[1]

Discussion at Leipsic (1519)

In 1519 a disputation was arranged at Leipsic between Carlstadt, an enthusiastic but not always very wise supporter of Luther, and John Eck, the papal champion. In the course of this discussion Luther caused an immense sensation by roundly declaring that the supremacy of the pope was unknown in the Scriptures, that it had grown up only in the previous 400 years, and that General Councils had erred in giving their support to it.

The die was now cast. The Reformer himself saw the full implications of his position. He freed himself for ever from the authority of popes, Fathers and Councils and henceforth took the Word of God as the only rule of faith. He stood before the world as a free Christian man, no longer subject to papal usurpation. The younger Humanists now rallied around Luther. The people of the German cities realized that, not only true religion, but the freedom of their country depended on his campaign. He seemed now to have the strength of a hundred men, and poured forth a

[1] See p. 84.

constant stream of sermons and pamphlets through the printing presses.

When Luther went to Leipsic he was accompanied by a bodyguard of 200 students and by Melanchthon, the young professor of Greek at Wittenberg. He became the fervent follower and life-long friend of Luther and finally his successor. They were complementary to one another—the calm learning and gentleness of Melanchthon standing over against the fiery passion and rugged boldness of Luther. As an expounder and systematizer of Protestant theology, Melanchthon became immensely popular and, when the great Reformer died, this brilliant follower succeeded him as leader of the Lutheran movement.

In 1520 Luther sent forth his three most famous pamphlets: *To the Nobility of the German Nation; Concerning Christian Liberty;* and *On the Babylonish Captivity of the Church.* They were nothing if not forcible in expression, and could hold the attention of even the most casual reader.

On June 15, 1520, came the pope's Bull excommunicating Luther and ordering his works to be burnt. The Reformer gave an appropriate reply. Having arranged a bonfire outside Wittenberg, he went arrayed in the robes of his Order, amid a crowd of sympathizers from the University and the town, and publicly flung the Bull, the Canon Law and the Forged Decretals into the fire. No gesture could have given a more emphatic message of defiance.

The Emperor Charles V and the Diet of Worms

The young emperor, Charles V, King of Spain, was at that time the most powerful monarch on earth, with vast territories throughout Europe and in the Americas. He was a fervent Roman Catholic and aimed at one big united Empire and one big united Church from which no one must dissent. He would willingly have extirpated the Protestants, but for two reasons he refrained. His constant wars with his enemy Francis I of France and the invasion of the Danube valley by the Turks meant that he needed the help of his Protestant subjects in his fight against these deadly foes.

In 1521 he called the imposing Diet of Worms, to which princes, dukes, prelates and other grandees were invited. His principal aim was to put down Luther, to whom, however, he gave a safe conduct. The Reformer's friends urged him not to go, for they remembered the fate of John Hus. The reply has never been forgotten: 'Though there were as many devils in Worms as tiles on its roofs, I would go.' The Diet, presided over by the emperor in person, was hostile. Luther was roughly questioned about his books and ordered to retract. Like Hus a century earlier, he declared he would retract nothing unless it were proved to be contrary to Scripture. His noble declaration: 'Here I stand. I can do no other. So help me God. Amen' has thrilled freedom-loving men through the centuries.

Owing to his having a safe conduct he was dismissed, but was condemned and placed under the ban of the Empire. To save his life, the Elector of Saxony secretly sent a troop of horsemen to arrest him on the way home. He was carried off to the castle of the Wartburg, and his enemies thought he had perished. In his confinement of nearly a year, he translated the New Testament from the original Greek into German—a work of supreme importance for the Reformation.

On his return to Wittenberg from the Wartburg in March 1522, Luther found the community in a frenzy of excitement because of the attacks of Carlstadt upon the rites and ordinances of the Church and the preaching of Claus Störch and other fanatics from Zwickau. The situation appeared to be very serious; but in eight days, Luther calmed the excited minds and restored order, thus keeping his movement in the paths of moderation.

The Revolt of the Nobles in 1523 and the Revolt of the Peasants in 1525 caused great distress to Luther and hampered his work. They were due to hard social and economic causes, but the Reformer was blamed. Luther foolishly urged the authorities to crush the Peasants' Revolt unmercifully, and many of his followers were alienated and a good number became Anabaptists.[1]

The Diets of Speier (1526 and 1529)

Having defeated his enemy, Francis I, and secured a promise of help in putting down Luther's followers, the emperor, Charles V, called the first Diet of Speier and ordered action to be taken against the Reformer's views. Strangely enough, he quarrelled seriously with the pope at the same time. The Diet, instead of condemning Luther, gave the famous edict of Speier in favour of toleration—that each state in Germany be allowed to hold the religion of its ruling prince. This principle of 'cuius regio, ejus religio' was finally accepted at the Peace of Augsburg in 1555.

The second Diet of Speier (1529) decided that the districts which had become Lutheran after the decisions of 1526 should remain so, but that the other districts should remain Catholic in perpetuity with no opportunity to introduce Reformed teaching. The evangelical minority in the Diet protested against the finding, because no Diet had the right to bind the consciences of men in matters of religion. Because of their protest they were called 'Protestants', and the origin of the term is worth noting. The Catholics formed a League to further the interests of their religion. Knowing that the intention of the emperor was to destroy Protestantism, the Elector of Saxony, the Landgrave of Hesse and other princes, formed a Protestant League, known as the League of Schmalkald, to resist aggression. It was most unfortunate that just at this

[1] See p. 115.

time, when the enemies of the Reformed cause were banding together in Germany to destroy it, a bitter conflict should have arisen between the Lutheran and Swiss theologians as to the meaning of the Lord's Supper. Philip of Hesse arranged a Conference in 1529 at Marburg with a view to settling the dispute. Complete agreement was secured on fourteen points. On the fifteenth point there was serious disunity. While all rejected the Roman Catholic doctrine of Transubstantiation as unscriptural, Luther believed in Consubstantiation, i.e. that Christ was present bodily in the bread and wine and asserted that the words 'This is my body' must be taken literally. Zwingli, the Swiss leader, held that the bread and wine were only signs which reminded men of the sacrifice of Christ, and that they fed on Him by faith. Luther was immovable and bitter. His intransigence caused incalculable loss to the Protestant cause.

Luther was initially so successful as a Reformer because he represented the spirit of the German people in their resistance to the abuses of the Roman Church, such as the scandals over Indulgences and the saying of Masses for the dead. The conviction was general that ecclesiastical reform was necessary and that men must get back to the simple faith of New Testament times. After the second Diet of Speier, however, and the formation of the Catholic League, Germany was irrevocably divided into Protestant and Catholic sections bitterly opposed to one another.

While Luther's work as a Reformer was of surpassing importance, he has been criticized for being too conservative in holding a doctrine of the Lord's Supper half-way between the Roman and the Zwinglian view, and at the same time retaining the crucifix, candles, Mass vestments and other elements characteristic of the Roman Catholic system. With regard to organization, he placed church power in the hands of the civil authorities as representing the Christian community.

The ruling princes in the large States, and the local councils in the free cities, appointed committees to manage ecclesiastical affairs and exercise church discipline. These committees were called consistories. The dominance of the civil power thus established in the German Church proved a source of spiritual weakness for generations.

THE ANABAPTISTS

This is the name given to certain groups of Christians who came into prominence about this time. They objected to infant baptism and rebaptized those who joined their communion. Hence the term. Reference has already been made to the excitement caused in Wittenberg in 1522 by Störch and other 'prophets' from Zwickau.[1] In that town a certain Thomas Münzer was closely associated with Störch and the 'prophets'. They preached a wild millenarianism and insisted that God's day of wrath was about to break and that the saints would dominate the governments of the world. They appealed strongly to the power of the sword to impose their views, and during their brief control of the city there were many excesses. In the past, most historians have represented these wild fanatics as being the founders of the Anabaptist movement. Research has shown that this view is undoubtedly erroneous. The real Anabaptists arose in Zürich, in 1522, among honourable men who called themselves 'Brethren' and were led by Conrad Grebel and Felix Manz. They laid great stress on Bible study, objected strongly to such a State Church as was countenanced by Luther and Zwingli, and asked for the removal of pictures and images from churches. They were men of sincere piety, and insisted that the Sword of the Spirit, the Word of truth, was their only weapon. They refused to recognize infant baptism.

During 1525 these views spread widely in the region

[1] See p. 112.

around Zürich. The Council of that city passed cruel and unjust laws against the Anabaptists. Unhappily, Zwingli was a party to these proceedings, and most of the leaders suffered the penalty of death. From 1525 to 1528 the movement became very strong in Germany, especially in Strasburg and Augsburg. Its members were often accused of being revolutionary and of plotting treasonable activities against the State, and were unjustly maligned in many ways. The Diet of Speier in 1529 approved an imperial mandate of the previous year that re-baptizers, and re-baptized, should be put to death even without proper forms of trial. It is reckoned that in a few years no less than two thousand perished. At first, Luther strongly opposed persecuting methods, but as the Anabaptist movement spread he became alarmed and, in 1530, urged 'the use of the sword against them by right of law'.[1] The movement continued to spread and increase, however. In the Netherlands, Menno Simons exercised much influence, and Jacob Hutter, a Tyrolese, did the same in Austria, Moravia and Poland, until his martyrdom in 1536. The Mennonite and Hutterite movements, which have done prominent work in many countries, including Russia, the United States, and Canada, took their designations from these men. They have always been pacific, earnest, and industrious Christians, and have often lived in communal settlements.

In view of the variations in teaching and practice which existed among the different Anabaptist groups, it is difficult to give a description of them which would cover all. Some of them, at least, inherited the traditions of certain of the anti-papal sects which abounded from the thirteenth century onwards. Generally speaking, they expected the speedy return of Christ, rejected completely the idea of a State Church, and possessed a boundless enthusiasm which sometimes carried them to extremes. The worst persecutions came from the

[1] James Mackinnon, *Luther and the Reformation*, IV, p. 64.

Roman Catholics, but, as we have seen, the Protestants were far from guiltless. Even John Calvin, though he did not persecute them, could see little good in them. The Anabaptists stood for religious liberty at a time when neither Protestants nor Catholics fully appreciated the importance of freedom of conscience. The Baptists, Quakers, and the Brethren, all have affinities with the Anabaptists, although none of them claim to have originated from them. The late Professor W. P. Paterson of Edinburgh admirably summed up the position with regard to them thus: 'It has been made clear that the Protestant tradition judged this movement by its worst examples, ignored the ethical idealism which entered into their dreams, and passed an anathema on all which was only merited by a few. It is, indeed, one of the tragedies of history that men like Hubmaier and Denck, and a great company of victims who followed them to the slaughter, should have been involved in the same condemnation with Münzer and John of Leyden.'[1]

[1] W. P. Paterson, *Rule of Faith*, p. 89.

CHAPTER XIV

THE REFORMATION IN SWITZERLAND

ULRICH ZWINGLI

WHILE Lutheranism spread from Germany into Denmark, Norway, and Sweden, and was eventually recognized as the State religion in these countries, there grew up in Switzerland a somewhat different type of Protestantism. Although the Reformation here lacked the dramatic incidents of the German movement, it was in reality more important. The Swiss type of the Reformed religion was more easily transplanted, and spread to France, Scotland, Hungary, Holland, a great part of Germany itself, to the English Puritans, to America, and to the British Dominions. The Swiss took their stand strongly on the Word of God as the only rule of faith and practice, and were not bound by so many mediaeval traditions as the early Lutherans. They swept away images, relics, pictures, pilgrimages and the use of the organ in public worship. Generally speaking, it may be said that the Reformation in Switzerland was very much more radical than in Germany.

Ulrich Zwingli (1484-1531), the leader of the Swiss Reformation, was a saint, scholar and patriot. He developed his ideas quite independently of Luther. On finishing a brilliant career at the Universities of Vienna and Basel he was appointed priest of Glarus and was later called to the great cathedral church of Zürich. He preached strongly against the corruption engendered among his countrymen through enlistment in foreign mercenary armies, including that of the pope, and also denounced the prevalent superstitions in the Church and the sale of Indulgences. Taking his stand on the Word of God, he fearlessly attacked in public disputation the distinctive doctrines of the Roman Church, and was supported strongly by the City Council of Zürich which set up an independent Church in 1522.

In 1528, the Reformation triumphed in Berne and St. Gall, and in 1529 at Basel, Mühlhausen, and Schaffhausen. All these became Protestant and republican, and carried out the political and religious reforms advocated by Zwingli. Very soon, he saw the impending danger from the five Forest Cantons which remained Roman Catholic and which had entered into a league with Ferdinand of Austria to destroy the Reformation. In spite of all his warnings to the Swiss and German Protestants as to the perils which threatened from this source, they failed to prepare. When Zürich was attacked by the Catholic Cantons, Zwingli died heroically with his people on the field of Cappel. He was a great Reformer but more radical in outlook than John Calvin, who was soon to appear as the outstanding leader of the Reformed Church.

JOHN CALVIN

Few men have suffered more from ignorant detraction than John Calvin. It would be well for some of those who condemn him out of hand to spend some little time studying his works. There is general agreement among serious scholars that Calvin was the greatest man of the Reformation era.

Born at Noyon, in Picardy, France, on July 10, 1509, he had good family connections and was educated among the nobility. He aroused remarkable affection in men so different from himself as Luther, Melanchthon, Bucer, and John Knox, even when they disagreed violently with him. His father first of all destined him for the priesthood, and then sent him to Orleans to study law. There, as formerly at Paris, he proved himself a most brilliant student. Under Humanist teachers his mind became steeped in classical learning. His legal training, coupled with the logical precision and clarity of mind so characteristic of the French, made him one of the most lucid and systematic theologians ever known, once he turned his attention to that field.

When his father died in 1532, Calvin returned from Orleans and joined a group of Protestants in Paris for the study of the Scriptures and for prayer. The following year he had to flee from Paris because of his evangelical views and the oration on 'Christian Philosophy' which he had written for his friend, Nicolas Cop, the Rector of Paris University. Passing through Strasburg, he was kindly received by Martin Bucer, one of the greatest scholars of the Reformation period, who was Professor of Theology in the university of that city. In 1535, Calvin settled in Basel as a refugee and continued his studies. In 1536 he published there his great work *The Institutes of the Christian Religion*. It was the first really systematic exposition of Reformed theology. Although much smaller than subsequent editions, it is safe to say that it was the ablest theological work ever written by a young man of twenty-six. As a presentation of Christian doctrine it has never been surpassed. It is of interest that its circulation has greatly increased within the last thirty years.

The work was based upon the Apostles' Creed and the aim was to show that Protestants were thoroughly loyal to this Creed and could not be regarded as heretics. Reformers like Luther and Calvin were giving no new Creed to the Church but were, instead, leading men back to the beliefs and practices of the apostolic age. Calvin more than any other man insisted that the Church must return again to the principles of the first three centuries, receiving the gospel in its simplicity.

When passing through Geneva in 1536, Calvin was visited by the local pastor, William Farel, who implored him in God's name to come to his help. In the previous year, the city had become formally Protestant. Political factors played a large part in this transformation, for the people wanted to be independent of the Duke of Savoy and the Bishop, who had formerly ruled them jointly. No moral or spiritual change had come over the community, which for long had been notorious for its licentiousness. Immoral doctrines were now entering under the guise of liberty. In despair, Farel appealed to Calvin to settle there. The latter was bent on devoting his life to literary work, but this seemed a call from God and he consented. Thus began the historic connection of Geneva with Calvinism.

Calvin immediately prepared articles of faith for the Church, a form of Church government, and a Catechism for the children. He proceeded to attack at the roots the licentiousness which was a disgrace to Geneva. Long before his arrival, the rulers of the city had made laws against gaming, drunkenness, masquerades, dances and extravagance in dress. As there was no change of heart, these laws proved unavailing. It is entirely erroneous to charge Calvin with the drawing up of such laws, and with vexatious interference in trivial matters affecting the private life of the citizens. Professor Lindsay has shown conclusively that every mediaeval town had such laws.

What Calvin rightly insisted on was that Church members should live in accordance with the demands of the New Testament. To secure this end, he asked that the Church should exercise its own discipline and debar from Communion unworthy members—what is now done in most Christian lands. Although he asked only for this small measure of spiritual independence, and the right to excommunicate flagrant and unrepentant sinners, the government of Geneva (supposed to be Protestant) rose in arms and expelled both Calvin and Farel. He went again to Strasburg where for three years he was pastor to the French refugees in a church where his name is still honoured and his tradition maintained. It was at this time that he became acquainted with both Luther and Melanchthon, and his near neighbour was Martin Bucer, who afterwards became Professor of Theology at Cambridge.

In Calvin's absence, matters deteriorated sadly in Geneva. Some of its citizens now realized that he was right in seeking a Church in which Christian law would rule. They saw, as he did, that infidelity was the root cause of their troubles. After various political conflicts, and when their freedom seemed in danger, the people of Geneva implored Calvin to return. He was very loth to do so as he had found a fruitful field of work at Strasburg. Only when he was pressed by his friends, and urged by Berne, Zürich and Basle, did he decide to go. He felt it was the will of God.

For twenty-four years he laboured in the city of his adoption. One feels amazed at the extent of his work —several sermons a week, a lecture every day, and a vast amount of correspondence with people all over Europe. He was the undoubted leader of the Protestant cause. No man had a more realistic conception of the needs of Europe in that day than Calvin. In face of the growing opposition of the Roman Church, he longed for a General Council of all Protestant Churches, but this he was unable to obtain owing to racial and theological prejudices.

Calvin stood up strongly for the principle that the Church members should elect office-bearers to carry on the government of the Church, and that in spiritual matters the Church must be independent of the State. He maintained, however, that the civil government was also a divine institution, and that Church and State should co-operate while respecting one another's separate spheres.

In 1541 the Ecclesiastical Ordinances set forth the laws by which the magistrates of Geneva dealt with

Church affairs. Pastors were to be elected by ministers already in office, and were to be appointed by the magistrates by consent of the people (who had only the right of veto). The elders were appointed by the City Council on the advice of the pastors. The pastors and elders together formed the Consistory which dealt with ecclesiastical affairs, and asked the civil authorities to impose penalties where necessary. There is much in these Ordinances contrary to what Calvin had earlier taught in the *Institutes* about the freedom of Christian people to elect their own Church office-bearers. It is obvious that in many things Calvin did not get his own way in Geneva, and he was not responsible for much that was done by the City Council and the Consistory. It was only in the French Protestant Church, and in Scotland, that Calvin's ideals as to Presbyterian church government found a free field, with most beneficial results. In this system nothing was to be introduced into the Church but what was positively sanctioned by the Word of God; the Church must conform to the New Testament pattern; its office-bearers (ministers and elders) must be elected by the Church members; and these are to rule the Church in presbyteries, synods and General Assemblies. Above all, Christ must be recognized as the only Head of the Church.

The central thought in Calvin's theology was the sovereignty of God. All things, therefore, which have to do with our salvation are founded on the will of God. We are saved only through the grace of God ministered to us by the Holy Spirit. God alone saves, not we ourselves. Hence, Calvin taught the doctrine of predestination and election. These are profound mysteries and were treated as such by Calvin himself. They are very perplexing but are undoubtedly taught in the Bible. All the other Reformers, including Luther, believed these doctrines, but it was Calvin who gave them logical consistency. It is easy to criticize them; it is not so easy to solve the tremendous questions involved.

Calvin always realized the vast importance of sound education and founded the College of Geneva with the illustrious Theodore Beza as head. Pastors from there passed to many lands and exercised a mighty influence in making known the reformed faith throughout Europe.

THE REFORMED CHURCH IN OTHER COUNTRIES

For reasons of space we can make only a passing reference to the Reformation in France, the Netherlands, Hungary, Spain and Italy.

In France, Lefèvre may be taken as the founder of the Protestant movement. Later, Calvin's influence became powerful and his views were adopted. For political reasons Francis I persecuted the Protestants at home and helped them abroad. Four thousand Waldenses,[1] belonging to that heroic body of evangelical Christians in northern Italy and southern France which dated back at least to 1170, were massacred in Provence in 1545. In spite of persecution the Protestants had 2,000 places of worship by 1558. On the night of August 24, 1572, came the diabolical massacre of St. Bartholomew, when, under the direction of the Queen Mother, Catherine de Medici, and the Guises, 2,000 were murdered in Paris, and 20,000 in the rest of France. Among them was the wise and noble Admiral Coligny and other great French leaders who were Protestants. It was not until 1598 that the French Protestants were granted religious freedom through the Edict of Nantes.

The Netherlands early gave a welcome to Calvinism, and the Reformed Church became strong. Philip II of Spain introduced the diabolical Inquisition in 1555, and it became an offence even to read the Bible. Beheading and burning became very common under this reign of terror until William the Silent, prince of

[1] See pp. 97, 125.

Orange, took up the fight for religious and civil freedom. In spite of the numerous executions carried on under the Duke of Alva, the gallant Netherlanders in 1572 formed the Utrecht Union, comprising the seven northern provinces which were Protestant, and laid the foundations of the Dutch nation. William was assassinated in 1584 by a Roman Catholic fanatic, but his work lived on.

In Hungary, Calvinism became the prevalent form of Protestantism. In spite of the hostility of the emperor Charles V in the sixteenth century, and severe persecutions by the Hapsburgs in the seventeenth, the movement could not be destroyed. In 1781 they were granted toleration, and by the nineteenth century had grown into the second largest Presbyterian Church in the world.

In spite of the Inquisition, Lutheran doctrines passed early into Spain and Italy and were accepted by a wide circle of cultured men. There were no finer Protestants than those of Spain. The movement, however, was completely stamped out by the Inquisition in 1559 and 1560. Much the same happened in Italy but there the Inquisition was less cruel although used freely by Pope Paul IV. Even bishops were suspected of harbouring Lutheran views in both Italy and Spain, and the situation seemed favourable for the reformed cause. Nevertheless, torture, imprisonment, and death almost destroyed Protestantism in these countries.

In the mountains and valleys of northern Italy, the Waldenses had survived since the twelfth century in spite of much bitter persecution. In 1532 they became a definite branch of the Reformed Church with a Presbyterian policy. They have struggled nobly for centuries, and since 1848 have enjoyed religious freedom.

CHAPTER XV

THE REFORMATION IN ENGLAND

THE BREAK FROM ROME

THE Reformation in England took a form very different from that on the Continent and in Scotland. It was carried out directly under Henry VIII who looked neither to Luther nor Calvin for a model. There is no reason to doubt that in his early days Henry was a sincere Roman Catholic who loved his Church. He entered the lists against Luther and wrote his treatise *On the Seven Sacraments* which brought him the title of 'Defender of the Faith' from a grateful pope. The fact that he broke with the Vatican in order to secure a divorce from Catherine of Aragon, to whom he had been married twenty-four years, has led to misrepresentation of the English Reformation in Roman Catholic countries where all the facts are not known. As a matter of justice, however, we must remember that Catherine was the widow of Henry's deceased brother, Arthur, and it was clearly against Scripture and Canon Law for the pope to grant in the first place a dispensation permitting the marriage. This was the emphatic opinion of Warham, Archbishop of Canterbury, and of every bishop in England except two. Many of the Universities of Europe held the same view. For political reasons, Ferdinand of Spain and Henry VII of England eagerly wanted the marriage and brought pressure to bear upon Prince Henry and Catherine, and even upon Pope Julius II, for to begin with all of them had scruples about it. The pressure from such powerful monarchs secured consent and the pope signed the dispensation allowing the marriage to take place. As all the children, except Mary, were still-born, and there was no son to carry on the Tudor line, Henry and others regarded it as a judgment for marrying his brother's widow.

By 1526 he had fallen in love with Anne Boleyn, and with Wolsey's help had applied to the pope for an annulment of his marriage with Catherine. To her credit, Anne courageously told the king she could not be his wife and would never be his mistress. Although the pope used his dispensing power freely when it suited him, he refused Henry's claim, not so much on moral grounds as for fear of Catherine's nephew, the emperor Charles V.

With the connivance of Parliament, Henry took steps in 1531 to dominate the situation. He boldly charged the English clergy with treason under the old Statute of 'Praemunire' which forbade receiving orders from a foreign power. In the province of Canterbury alone they were fined £100,000. The following year, with the help of Parliament, the king secured the abject 'submission' of the clergy. Henceforth, the Church of England was under his control.

In spite of his being unpopular at the Vatican, Cranmer was made Archbishop of Canterbury in 1532 when Henry threatened to stop the despatch of 'annates'[1] to Rome. Next year, Parliament passed the famous Act of Restraint of Appeals to stop all appeals to the Holy See. Henry secretly married Anne Boleyn. Later, Archbishop Cranmer tried the question of the divorce before his own court, and declared the marriage with Catherine null and void. The pope fulminated and ordered the faithful to resist Henry, but in vain. This led to the definite break with the Church of

[1] The *annates* represented a year's income claimed by the pope on the death of a bishop, abbot or parish priest, and paid by his successor.

Rome in 1534. Of many Acts passed then, the most important was the Supremacy Act by which the king was declared to be the 'Supreme Head of the Church of England'. It became treason to call the king a heretic. Very interesting is the declaration made by the two Houses of Convocation that 'the Roman Pontiff has no greater jurisdiction bestowed on him by God in the Holy Scriptures than any other foreign bishop'.

At first the change in England could scarcely be called a Reformation. Matters remained virtually as before, except that now the king was Head of the Church, not the pope. At the same time, there were some very hopeful factors. There was a strong desire for reform latent in the hearts of the English people. Without this, not even the ruthless and despotic Henry could have brought about the separation from Rome. For centuries many had strongly resented the intervention of the pope, whom they regarded as a foreign potentate, in the affairs of England, and this was reflected in the legislation of the country. From the days of Wyclif not a few had read the Scriptures in their own language and were openly critical of the Roman Church. Many objected to paying tithes to the priests, and in particular to paying 'annates' and 'Peter's pence' to the pope.

There was much private piety of an evangelical kind in the land even before Luther's day. Men like Cranmer, Thomas Cromwell, and Latimer came to have strong Protestant leanings. But most bishops, while wishing for a reform in conduct, still wanted to retain the theology and practice of the Roman Church. In 1536 the king himself prepared Ten Articles of Religion. They claimed to be based on the Bible and the Ancient Creeds, but still retained Roman Catholic elements as regards baptism and the Real Presence.

'Injunctions' were issued in 1536 and 1538, warning against unnecessary holy days and against the abuse of images, relics, and supposed priestly miracles. It was a great step forward when it was ordered that a large Bible should be placed in each church and that the people be encouraged to read it. What was not taught in Scripture was to be avoided such as 'pilgrimages, offering money or candles to images . . . and saying prayers over beads'. The Church was obviously moving in the right direction; but there were setbacks such as when the bishops prepared a manual called *The Bishop's Book* which was reactionary and recognized Seven Sacraments. The greatest gain was the place given to the Scriptures. The Church owes an unspeakable debt to the scholarly William Tyndale in this connection. His translation of the Bible was epoch-making. When condemned and persecuted at home, he carried on his work on the Continent; and, in spite of the most bitter opposition, sent his translations in great quantities into England and Scotland. He was burnt in Brabant in 1536.

The dissolution of the monasteries in 1536 and 1539, and the sale of the lands cheaply to his courtiers, brought Henry large revenues and established an upper middle class which ever since then has had a great influence in English life. When the king realized that the Reformation was moving too fast for public sentiment, he became violently reactionary. To deny Transubstantiation or to say that a priest or nun might marry, meant burning. Thomas Cromwell was executed and Bishop Latimer was sent to prison. Both Protestants and Romanists who differed from Henry were hurried to execution. When he died in 1547, England was in a ferment, some wanting the new ideas, others wishing to adhere to the mediaeval system.

THE REFORMATION UNDER EDWARD VI (1547-1553)

This young king was only ten when he ascended the throne. He was a youth of genuine piety and a frank and avowed friend of the Reformation, due in no small measure to Archbishop Cranmer's training. The cruel

Six Articles of Henry VIII, and other repressive legislation, were swept away and the people became free to
form their own views on doctrine. The Lord's Supper
was now observed in Protestant fashion, and the clergy
were allowed to marry. The publication of the First
Prayer-Book of Edward VI in 1549 was a great step
forward. The whole service was now in English for the
first time, and the new Prayer-Book had to be used in
every church.

Because of the change in attitude, refugees returned
from the Continent. They included men like Ridley
and Hooper, who had been under the influence of such
continental Reformers as Zwingli and Bullinger. They
were helped by Cranmer, who was now a thorough-
going Protestant, and men of the type of Hooper,
Ridley, Coverdale, Ponet, and Scory were made bishops.

In 1547, Charles V had gained a great victory over
the German Protestants at Muhlberg, and as a result
the position of many Reformed Church leaders on the
Continent became perilous. Among those who fled to
England was Martin Bucer of Strasburg, the friend of
Calvin, who became Professor of Theology at Cambridge, Paul Buchlin, a brilliant Hebrew scholar, and
the great Italians, Peter Martyr and Bernardino
Ochino. One of the most interesting was John a Lasco
(or Laski), a Polish nobleman, who had become a great
theologian and fervent supporter of the Reformed
Church. He was destined to exercise a profound influence upon religious life in England.

The British people are, indeed, debtors to all these
refugees. They greatly strengthened the hands of those
who maintained that the Reformation in England was
incomplete and that too much of the discipline, ritual,
and ceremonial of the Roman Church still remained.
They wanted to model the Anglican Church on the
pattern of continental Protestantism, especially on
that of Geneva. Those who took up this attitude were
known as Puritans. In later years the name was applied

specially to those of their number who practised austerity and strictness in religious matters. Since the continental refugees, for political reasons, were allowed to have a congregation of their own in London, free from governmental interference, their church became a rallying ground for the Puritans in times of opposition.

There was great need for the ecclesiastical changes brought about by the Protectorate. Shortly before the death of Henry VIII, Bishop Hooper had written: 'The impious Mass, the most shameful celibacy of the clergy, the invocation of saints, auricular confession, superstitious abstinence from meats and purgatory, were never before held by the people in greater esteem.'[1] A new set of 'Injunctions' was now sent out for the guidance of the clergy. They are illuminating as to the condition of the Church. Ministers were not to 'extol or set forth any images, relics, or miracles'. They were instructed to preach 'four times a year', which shows how preaching had fallen into desuetude in the Roman Church. On every holy day the clergy were to recite 'openly and plainly' from the pulpit the Lord's Prayer, the Creed, and the Ten Commandments in English 'to the intent the people may learn the same by heart'.

They were enjoined 'not to frequent taverns or ale houses, not to give themselves to drinking or riot, or spend their time idly at dice, cards, tables or gaming', a sad reflection on their spiritual condition.

In 1552 came the Second Prayer-Book of Edward VI, the aim of which was to make the worship of England more like that of the continental Reformed Churches and less like the Church of Rome. The Communion service was made definitely Protestant. The word 'table' is used instead of 'altar', which is highly significant. The terms 'minister' and 'priest' are interchangeable, and officiating clergy are forbidden to use 'Alb, Vestment, or Cope'. The preparation of the

[1] *Zurich Letters*, 36.

Prayer-Book was principally the work of Cranmer. In it we see a manifestation of his deeply devotional spirit and his mastery of the English language. He made succeeding generations his debtors. In the words of Bishop J. C. Ryle, 'People were taught that justification was by faith without the deeds of law, and that every heavy-laden sinner on earth had a right to go straight to the Lord Jesus Christ for remission of sins, without waiting for pope or priest, confession or absolution, masses or extreme unction.' This Second Prayer-Book is important because the present Prayer-Book is essentially the same.

In spite of the lack of political acumen in the Protector, Somerset, and glaring weaknesses in other members of the Council, a most salutary change came over the religious condition of the people during the short reign of Edward. The response of the people, in the cities at least, showed that they were wearied to death of the cruel Romanism under his own headship which Henry VIII had favoured.

THE ROMAN CHURCH RE-ESTABLISHED UNDER MARY
(1553-1558)

The Reformation was perhaps beginning to move too fast for some when the pious young monarch died on July 6, 1553. He was succeeded by his half-sister, Mary Tudor, daughter of Catherine of Aragon, who, like her Spanish mother, was a fanatical Romanist. Her great aim was to bring England back to the Catholic fold. The misgovernment of Somerset and Northumberland in the previous reign made this easier because of the discontent which it had aroused.

One of Mary's first acts (August 18, 1553) was to prohibit all preaching and printing without her licence, thus striking a blow at all Protestant work. Soon the great Protestant bishops, like Cranmer, Ridley, Coverdale, Hooper and Latimer, were lodged in prison, and bishops loyal to Rome took their place.

In 1554, the queen married her cousin Philip II of Spain, son of the emperor Charles V. It was part of the scheme to bring all Christendom within the orbit of Spanish power and under the ecclesiastical guidance of the papacy. The marriage was most unpopular in England and proved very unhappy for Mary and Philip themselves.

On November 30, 1554, the Lords and Commons, on royal instigation, presented a Supplication 'that they might receive absolution, and be received into the body of the Holy Catholic Church, under the pope, the Supreme Head thereof'. Cardinal Pole, the new legate in England, was graciously pleased to grant this absolution, the Queen and Philip, and the Lords and Commons, receiving it on bended knees. It was a humiliating spectacle. The pope, and not the sovereign, was now once more Head of the Church in England.

The former laws against heretics were revived, and the old Roman Catholic ceremonies were brought back. Terrible persecution began. Bishops Bonner and Gardiner stand out as cruel and insatiable in their lust for blood. The first to perish was John Rogers, Prebendary of St. Paul's, to whom Tyndale had entrusted the great work of completing his translation of the Bible. His fate evoked great sympathy and vast crowds cheered him as he went to execution. Within five days, Bishop Hooper, the great Puritan Bishop, who had protested against the use of vestments, was burnt in his cathedral town of Gloucester on February 9, 1555. God had blessed his work, and his devoted people were deeply moved by his death.

The British people have never forgotten the martyrdom of Bishops Ridley and Latimer, who were burnt at Oxford in front of Balliol College on October 16, 1555, for denying Transubstantiation and the sacrifice of the Mass. The words of Latimer to Ridley as they faced the flames were prophetic: 'Be of good cheer,

Master Ridley, and play the man; we shall this day, by God's grace, light such a torch in England as will never be put out.' Archbishop Cranmer was not burnt at Oxford until March 21, 1556. In a moment of weakness and under terrible pressure which momentarily broke him down, he had signed a recantation of his views. He made ample amends for his weakness. In the church, on the morning of his martyrdom, he bore an unflinching testimony before his enemies. At the stake he showed the world his sorrow for signing the document. He threw it in the flames, pleading for God's pardon and the forgiveness of the people, and urging them to maintain the doctrines he had taught. He then held the offending hand and arm in the flames until they were burnt to a cinder.

Mary deposed at least 1,200 clergymen for being married men. In her short reign no less than 286 were burnt for being Protestants, besides 'those that dyed of famyne in sondry prisons'. A multitude suffered imprisonment and the spoiling of their goods. It was no wonder the people called the Queen 'Bloody Mary'. Her life was indeed one of tragedy. Forgetting the brightness of her youth she became ever more embittered, and ended her life one of the most disappointed and miserable of women—hated even by her husband and at variance with the pope whose cause she had served with unbounded devotion.

QUEEN ELIZABETH AND THE PURITANS

The accession of Queen Elizabeth in 1558 brought immense joy to multitudes, for persecution now ceased. Protestant exiles returned from abroad and congratulated the new queen. Even the returning Puritan[1] leaders were given a place in the reconstituted church. Elizabeth, however, disliked the theology of Geneva, and this was soon shown in her treatment of the Puritans. She missed a great opportunity of making the

[1] For a definition of Puritanism see pp. 150 ff.

Church of England a really national and united Church, for a few concessions then would probably have retained the Puritans in the National Church for all time.

In the eyes of the Vatican, Queen Elizabeth was illegitimate, for the pope had never recognized the divorce of her father from Catherine of Aragon. In the opinion of the Roman Church, her cousin, Mary Queen of Scots, was the legal heir to the English throne. In spite of Elizabeth's love of Romish pomp and ceremony, she was compelled to fall back upon Protestants for her bishops. She could not look to France or Spain for help, because both strongly favoured Mary of Scotland on religious grounds. In France, Mary's uncles, the Duke of Guise and the Cardinal of Lorraine were very powerful. Elizabeth was thus compelled to maintain an Anglican Church. She was careful to exercise her full power as Supreme Governor of the Church, and kept its management in her own hands.

The Acts against heretics under which so many Protestants were burnt in Mary's time were repealed. A Commission recommended that the Second Prayer-Book of Edward VI be adopted once more. It was rather too Protestant for Queen Elizabeth, and from the proceedings in Convocation it is clear that the clergy were prepared to go much further in the matter of reform than she was. She insisted that the law concerning vestments and ornaments should be as in the Prayer-Book of 1549, which was much less Protestant than that of King Edward's Second Prayer-Book in 1552. She also insisted on certain alterations being made in the proposed Articles as to the Communion, in order to bring it somewhat nearer to the Lutheran position. The queen was imperious and had her way, but fortunately the changes made in the proposed Articles were not considerable. Taking them all in all, the Thirty-Nine Articles agreed to in 1562 are a magnificent statement of Reformed doctrine and have made for stability in the religious life of England. The degree to which the doctrine of the Church of England (as established in the reign of Elizabeth) was Calvinist is remarkable. Even on the matter of the Communion there was practical agreement with Geneva as shown by the revised Articles XXVIII and XXIX.

The Act of Supremacy of 1559 made the queen Supreme Governor of the Church of England; and the Act of Uniformity of the same year made it obligatory for all to join in one public worship according to the rules laid down. This was productive of dissensions afterwards, as was the Ornaments Rubric introduced by Elizabeth into the Prayer-Book, whereby rites and ceremonies could be increased.

The queen was blessed with very wise counsellors, of whom William Cecil was chief. These urged the importance of helping the Dutch and the Huguenots, as well as the Protestant party in Scotland. It was no easy task to get her to give her support to these, for she disliked the Genevan doctrine, and in particular, she hated John Knox. Finally, however, help was given. On her attitude to the Puritans, Professor A. F. Mitchell writes: 'What Froude has said of Knox may be said in a measure of his Puritan brethren in England: that they saved Elizabeth's throne and secured the triumph of Protestantism in Britain, in spite of herself, and all her caprice and cruelty towards them.'[1] These were the men who could be relied upon, not the Marian clergy who could change from one religion to another so easily. Ignoring this fact, Queen Elizabeth set herself sternly to repress what were called 'prophesyings'. These were gatherings of ministers and godly people to study the Scriptures, and already they had been greatly blessed. They were cordially supported by the good Archbishop Grindal. He refused to carry out the queen's command to suppress them, and as a result was suspended and imprisoned in his own house.

[1] A. F. Mitchell, *Westminster Assembly*, p. 44.

At this time, Thomas Cartwright, the great Puritan and Presbyterian divine, comes into prominence. A distinguished Fellow of St. John's College, Cambridge, he was appointed Lady Margaret Professor of Divinity in Cambridge, in succession to Archbishop Whitgift who became an enemy of the Puritans. Puritanism was exceedingly strong at Cambridge, a fact which greatly displeased the queen. Cartwright was very popular, and his lectures caused a ferment in the University. In spite of the support of the great minister Cecil, and the favourite Leicester, Whitgift persuaded Her Majesty to remove him from his chair in 1570. According to Cartwright the Church was entitled to regulate its doctrine, polity, and worship by the Word of God without restriction by the State; the head of the Commonwealth was only a member of the Church, not its Governor; and Episcopacy, as then known in England, was of human growth. These were the principles afterwards adopted in the Westminster Assembly in the seventeenth century. Indeed, Cartwright's Directory for Church Government was carefully studied in that Assembly. In spite of being one of the most learned men in Europe, and one of the most pious, he was cruelly treated, and twice had to flee from his native land. In his old age he died almost in obscurity at Warwick, in 1603. Nevertheless, his influence on the Puritan movement was very far-reaching.

While Queen Elizabeth could control the Church, she found a majority of the House of Commons against her. They were led by two strong Christian men, Strickland and Wentworth, who favoured the Puritans. The conflict was severe and was the beginning of that contest between Crown and Parliament which was to issue in the Civil War of the seventeenth century and the overthrow of the Stuart dynasty.

In 1571 there was passed an Act which acknowledged the validity of ordination by Presbyters, without a bishop. While it demanded acceptance by the clergy of the doctrinal part of the Thirty-Nine Articles, it did not bind them to the constitution or ritual. This is how the Presbyterians were able to remain inside the National Church until driven out at the Restoration in 1660.

Queen Elizabeth carried out her arbitrary will through the bishops, the Star Chamber, and the Court of High Commission. When Archbishop Grindal would not proceed against the 'prophesyings' she did it herself. Cases like the proceedings against the writers of the Marprelate Tracts which had attacked Prelacy roused intense feeling in the land, and the cruel sentences on Penry and Udall, Puritan propagandists who were hanged, turned many against the sovereign. The very name of the Star Chamber became an abomination in the eyes of the people, and Elizabeth became very unpopular. The feeling grew up in the hearts of many that civil and religious liberty must be fought for and this finally blazed up against Charles I in the Civil War of the next century.

Elizabeth regained the love of her subjects in an eminent degree during the dangerous time of the invasion by the Spanish Armada in 1588. In those perilous days she seemed to embody all that was best in the nation. In her faith and strength and courage, she stands forth as a noble figure. For years the pope, and the kings of Spain and France, had done everything possible to overturn her régime. She was excommunicated, and her Catholic subjects were encouraged to revolt. On Mary Queen of Scots centred innumerable intrigues aiming at the removal of Elizabeth with foreign help. English priests were specially trained at Douay and other places on the Continent with the express intention of leading England and Scotland once more into allegiance to the papacy. Elizabeth was compelled for her own defence to send help openly to the Netherland Protestants in their gallant fight against Philip II of Spain. Meanwhile, Sir Francis

Drake harried Philip's ships on the Spanish main in exploits which have become almost legendary.

In 1588, Philip resolved to carry out the invasion of England of which he had dreamt for years. The Spaniards proudly named the great Armada 'the Invincible'. It numbered 160 ships with some 30,000 marines and sailors and was far more powerful than the English fleet. At Calais was a strong army with everything ready to cross to England. The superb seamanship of the English admirals, and their novel tactics, coupled with the boundless heroism of their men, won a glorious victory in the Channel. Storms did the rest, and the Armada was scattered through the North Sea and wrecked on the coasts of England, Norway, and Scotland. Many felt it was the doing of the Lord. It was a great deliverance for Protestantism, and a shattering blow for Spain. Henceforth her power was on the wane.

In spite of her Tudor obstinacy and autocracy, Elizabeth was a great queen. The foundations of England's civil and religious greatness were solidly laid in her reign. To the men of that age we owe much. In the words of a nineteenth-century Christian historian, 'They made England independent of an Italian priest-prince. They freed the land from monks and monkery. They abolished that most fruitful source of immorality, the celibacy of the clergy, and made laymen and ecclesiastics alike subject to the civil courts.

'They exploded the doctrine of purgatory—that richest mine of priestly wealth and popular superstition. They removed from between the soul and God the crowd of priests and saintly mediators, and taught men to go to Christ rather than to the Blessed Virgin or the glorified dead.'[1]

---

[1] Cunningham Geekie, *The English Reformation*, p. 503.

CHAPTER XVI

THE REFORMATION IN SCOTLAND

IN no other country in the world was the Reformation so complete or so thorough as in Scotland. It is also remarkable that in this small country, with its turbulent history, the Reformation was carried through with virtually no loss of life to the Roman Catholics and with very few imprisonments. This was due to such historical factors as: (1) the precious spiritual legacy left by the old Celtic Church; (2) the influence of Lollardy brought back from Oxford by Scottish students; (3) the teachings of John Hus, of Peter Dubois, and William of Occam brought home by many Scottish travellers and students on the Continent; (4) the steady percolation of Lutheran ideas; (5) the well-known depravity of the Catholic clergy which had become a byword and revealed the need for reform.

Scotland was profoundly moved by the martyrdom of the high-born and saintly Patrick Hamilton in 1528. Returning home at the end of 1527, he fearlessly preached the gospel of God's grace. Under the guise of friendship he was invited by Archbishop Beaton to a conference and was then charged with heresy and burnt in front of St. Salvator College, St. Andrews, on February 29, 1528. His death produced a mighty impression throughout the land. 'The reek (i.e. smoke) of Master Patrick Hamilton infected as many as it blew upon.' Eighteen years later, that gentle, handsome, and Spirit-filled man, George Wishart, was betrayed into the hands of Cardinal Beaton and, after a mock trial, was put to death in the same city on the latter's own responsibility, contrary to the Regent's orders. The spirit of the nation was deeply stirred by this shameless proceeding. Many felt the time for resistance had come.

On May 29, 1546, Norman Leslie (Master of Rothes), Kirkcaldy of Grange and others, forced their way into the Castle of St. Andrews, early in the morning, slew the cardinal, and hanged his body out of the window. These men never came to be closely associated with the Reformation, and their action was chiefly due to political motives and personal bitterness. After the death of Patrick Hamilton, inquisition had been constantly made for those who had New Testaments or who professed Reformed doctrines. Some were burnt, others sentenced to severe punishment, and many fled. In spite of the burnings, the Reformed views spread more and more. The clergy, both secular and regular, were held up to ridicule all over the land in plays and satires condemning their vicious lives, as in the writings of Sir David Lyndsay of the Mount, and George Buchanan, the world-renowned classical scholar. It was not until John Knox arose, however, that the widespread Protestant sentiment was brought into focus. As soon as he preached his first sermon in the Castle of St. Andrews, which was then in Protestant hands, people said, 'Other men sned (sawed) the branches of the Papistry. This man lays his axe to the trunk of the tree.' It was true. He was, indeed, a strong man.

Scotland was in a sadly disjointed state, virtually ruled by the French under Mary of Guise, who had a French army in Edinburgh and Leith. The young queen, married to the Dauphin and living in France, was under the influence of her Guise uncles whose fanaticism went beyond all bounds. The European political situation was very tense. Scotland's relationships with England, France, and Spain were all dangerous, and served further to affect the rising Protestant cause. If only the Roman Catholics could retain Scotland they could use it as a base for the destruction of Protestant England. For a time the little kingdom of Scotland was politically the most important spot in Europe.

No other man could have guided the Church in Scotland as Knox did in that stormy and critical period, when the most violent passions were wildly warring in Church and State, and when the Council of Trent had aroused intense fanaticism. It is all very well to criticize the Scottish Reformer for his sternness and alleged roughness. Only a man of unyielding mould could have grappled with the situation, for he was surrounded by the diabolical elements of war, intrigue, deception and murder. In spite of his sternness, there are not lacking evidences of a kinder and even a lovable disposition. Above all, he was a man who feared God and that cast out other fear. He was always at his best in a great emergency when the hearts of other men were failing them. Then his strong qualities shone out.

The training which this great man received for his tremendous task suggests a divine providence. After receiving a good university education at Glasgow under teachers like the famous John Major, he trained as a priest and papal notary. Then he spent nineteen months as a slave in the French galleys after the capture by the French fleet of St. Andrews Castle. Next we find him for five years labouring in England in the reign of Edward VI, when Scotland was still groaning under the thraldom of Rome. During this period he met many outstanding Church leaders, such as Latimer, Ridley, Hooper, and Miles Coverdale, men who wholeheartedly accepted the Reformed point of view as presented by Geneva. Cranmer was his friend, and Knox became one of the king's preachers. His association with these good and true men in England moulded his own outlook. He was offered the bishopric of Rochester, but declined it because of his views on Church polity.

When, on the accession of Mary Tudor, he had to flee from England this too worked out for good. In Frankfort, as minister of the English-speaking congregation, he learned to appreciate good men and to deal with unreasonable and tricky ones. At Geneva, he was the intimate friend of John Calvin and Theodore Beza. He had the benefit of seeing the Reformed Church in action within a thoroughly Protestant community. Above all, he saw at work the master mind of Calvin taking the Bible as the Word of God and systematizing its truths in a doctrinal framework such as had never been seen before. Thus it was that when he returned to Scotland in 1559 he was well equipped in every way for his tremendous task. By 1560 the Roman Church had virtually vanished out of the land.

On the political side, the cause of the Reformation was enormously strengthened by the alliance between England and Scotland, which was made in the Treaty of Berwick (May, 1560). By the Treaty of Cateau—Cambrésis (April, 1559), the kings of France and Spain had bound themselves to crush Protestantism in Europe. The danger was very real. Urged on by Throckmorton, the English Ambassador at Paris, who saw the peril looming ahead, William Cecil, with extreme difficulty, finally succeeded in persuading Queen Elizabeth to enter into an alliance with the Protestants of Scotland. An English fleet sailed into the Forth; the French troops were surrounded in the fort at Leith, and soon France had lost her hold on Scotland. For the first time in history, an English army was cheered as it marched through the streets of Edinburgh.

At the request of Parliament, John Knox and five friends drew up a statement of the Reformed doctrine. Although it constituted a fair-sized book, they drew up this Scots Confession in four days, a truly astonishing performance. It was approved by the Scottish Parliament with very great enthusiasm and remained in force as the symbol of Scottish religion until 1647 when it was replaced by the Westminster Confession of Faith. Knox and his friends were also asked to draw up a statement as to how the Church should be governed. The result was the First Book of Discipline which expounded the Presbyterian method of Church polity, a system which makes for balance and good order. Knox also set forth at this time a magnificent scheme for the education of the people, his ideal being to have 'a kirk and a school in every parish'. In the Book of Discipline it was insisted that the properties and vast revenues of the old Church should be reserved for the maintenance of religion, education and the poor. Because of this, Parliament refused to ratify it, for the greedy nobles grasped as much as they could of the patrimony of the Church, to the great loss of the people of Scotland. Knox's ideal, however, was never lost sight of.

A year before Mary Queen of Scots returned from France (on August 19, 1561), the Reformation had been thoroughly established. John Knox and the nobles, who were aware of the atmosphere in which Mary had been reared at the Court of France, knew what to expect. Her aim was to gain time at first so as to strengthen her position. Then she would strike a blow for the elimination of Protestantism. On the very first Sunday after her return she had Mass said by a French priest at the palace of Holyrood House. Her personality fascinated one after another of the nobles, but she could never move John Knox. Queen Mary stood for an alliance with autocratic France and Romanism; John Knox stood for Presbyterianism, democracy, and alliance with England. The two ideals were utterly incompatible and a clash was inevitable.

No other man knew so clearly as Knox the issues at stake. Let it be remembered in relation to their disputes, that he never visited the palace except when summoned by the queen; that he was deferential as a subject, and that before the end of her reign, Mary showed him no small sign of friendship when she invited him to visit her at Lochleven Castle. This last meeting was pleasant to both. The truth is that this young and charming queen, who could dissemble so easily, was held from childhood in the grip of an evil system. She was a martyr to what she had been taught, and her own impulsiveness in throwing herself away on worthless husbands brought about her downfall, and surrounded her with a pathos which will never be forgotten.

After the death of Knox, first the Regents and then the young king, James VI, did their best to undermine Presbyterianism and establish Episcopacy. James followed a very tortuous policy; at one time extolling the Presbyterian Church as the finest Church in Christendom, and at another endeavouring to shackle it and turn it into a prelatical church, and a tool of the Court, according as political exigencies seemed to demand. His great aim was to secure at all costs the throne of England on the death of Elizabeth. Andrew Melville, Principal first of Glasgow University and then of St. Andrews, arose as the great defender of the Presbyterian Church system. King James was a most shifty and unsatisfactory man, and Melville had the temerity to tell him to his face that there were two kings and two kingdoms in Scotland—the kingdom of the Lord Jesus Christ where James was only a subject, and the civil kingdom where James was the sovereign. Although in 1592 Melville gained a very great victory for the Presbyterian system, when both Parliament and king recognized amply the claims of the Church of Scotland, and passed an Act guaranteeing all its rights and privileges and its Presbyterian polity, yet by 1597, King James, through his duplicity had put an end to free assemblies. The next development was the restoration of Episcopacy, and the Church of Scotland was brought into bondage to the Court until 1638.

CHAPTER XVII

THE COUNTER-REFORMATION

THE COUNCIL OF TRENT

FOR at least a century it had been felt everywhere in Europe, outside the Roman Curia, that a reform of abuses in the Catholic Church was a clamant necessity. In 1545, the emperor Charles V, constantly disturbed by the religious difficulties in Germany, persuaded Pope Paul III to call the Council of Trent. It met at intervals from 1545 to 1563. The emperor looked for reforms and a reconciliation with the German Lutherans; but the Council was predominantly Italian and under the control of the pope, and the emperor failed to influence it.

The reactionary party under Caraffa (afterwards Pope Paul IV) gained a complete victory, and guided the Church skilfully into a fanatical path which led to fresh vitality and prestige after the shattering blows received at the Reformation. The Papal Legate was horrified at the request of the Protestants that all the decisions of the Council should be tested by their agreement with Scripture. The Council declared the Latin Vulgate to be the only authoritative version of the Bible, and they received 'with an equal feeling of piety and reverence the traditions'—although no one seemed very clear where these traditions were lodged. It was further enacted that every Catholic must accept the interpretation of Scripture given by the Church.

The dogmas set forth left no doubt as to the position of the Roman Church in regard to doctrine, and strongly reiterated the views held before the Reformation. The view of the Curia prevailed as to the pope's position of authority in the Church. It was enacted that all clergy must swear 'I acknowledge the Holy Catholic Apostolic Roman Church for the mother and mistress of all Churches; and I promise and swear true obedience to the Bishop of Rome, successor to St. Peter, Prince of Apostles, and Vicar of Jesus Christ'.

At Trent a number of abuses were remedied and the education of priests was improved. Discipline was tightened, and in these ways the Roman Church became a more compact and effective instrument for the fight with Protestantism.

THE JESUITS

We cannot understand modern church history without knowing something about the Society of Jesus, the Order initiated by Ignatius Loyola in 1534. In 1521 this dashing and very heroic young Spanish officer was badly wounded. In hospital, he passed through a great spiritual change, whereupon he adopted a hermit's life of extreme asceticism involving sufferings so severe that they changed his appearance. He believed he had visions of the devil, and of Christ and His saints battling against the prince of darkness. In his broodings he decided 'some entirely new foundation pillars' must be found unless the whole Roman Church were to perish. He resolved to fight against the teachings of the Reformers. Resuming again the polished life of an aristocrat, he founded at Paris the Society of Jesus with six friends. They bound themselves by solemn oaths to be 'true spiritual knights' and to extend 'the true faith among believers'. It was felt by the pope that here was an Order which could help the Roman Church to recover from its losses in the Reformation. In lands like Spain and Italy, where the Catholics were in a big majority, the Inquisition could wipe out the Protestants. Where, however, these latter were numerous, it was better for the Jesuits to infiltrate and, by suavity of manners, ingratiate themselves with the influential classes and lead back the people to the Roman fold. According to Nicolini, the Jesuit was 'despotic in Spain, constitutional in England, republican in Paraguay, bigot in Rome, idolater in India'.

The discipline of the Order was most rigorous and exacting. The *Spiritual Exercises*, a book binding on every member, laid down: 'That we may be entirely of the same mind with the Church, if she have defined anything black which may appear to our minds to be white, we ought to believe it to be as she has pronounced it.' The acceptance of this teaching put men into spiritual slavery in relation to their ecclesiastical superiors.

To further the interests of the Roman Church, Loyola taught the Order that 'it is permissible to do evil that good may come', a principle which led to unspeakable wickedness. In dealing with ethical questions, the Jesuits developed a system of casuistry and sophistry which brought them into disrepute in many quarters. The Parliament of Paris in 1762 declared that their doctrines 'tended to sever all the bonds of civil society by the authorization of falsehood, perjury, the most culpable impurity, and in a word, each passion and each crime of human weakness'.

The Jesuits became the life and soul of the Counter-Reformation, their influence being very powerful in the Council of Trent in its last years. They specialized in education and established flourishing schools all over Europe, where young people were turned into eager instruments for promoting the designs of the Vatican. Everywhere the Jesuits were active—among outcasts in the cities, in preaching, in personal dealing. Meanwhile the bloody engine of the Inquisition was set in motion wherever it would work. In one way or another the Roman Church won back much territory lost in southern Germany, Austria and Bohemia. The plots and intrigues of the Jesuits were numerous in many countries. We find them intriguing in England in Queen Elizabeth's time and in Scotland in the days of Queen Mary and James VI. Their schemes sometimes included plans for the assassination of their opponents, including the highest in the land.

In connection with the Counter-Reformation, we notice the zeal and self-sacrifice of Francis Xavier (1506-1552), and other Roman Catholic missionaries. Xavier, a Jesuit and friend of Loyola, claimed that in his ten years' work in Goa (India), Malacca, the Moluccas and other East Indian islands, and in Japan, he baptized no less than 700,000 converts. There are indications that the work was somewhat superficial and the Jesuits were afterwards severely censured by other Roman Catholic Orders for accommodating themselves too much to heathen customs and practices. This led to the break-up of the Jesuit Missions.

So glaring became the intrigues and plots of the Jesuits in later years that they were banished or suppressed in nearly every Roman Catholic country, including Spain and Portugal with their vast territories in America, France, Naples, and Parma. To crown all, in 1773, Pope Clement XIV abolished the Order. He referred to the vexations suffered at their hands by some of his predecessors in the papal chair, and called attention to 'the complaints and cries' raised against them, and 'the dangerous results, rebellions and scandals' which followed on their doings, and tells how the faithful Catholic kings of Spain, France, Portugal, and the Sicilies were constrained to banish the Order 'to prevent Christ being seized and torn out of the lap of the Holy Mother Church'. For forty years the Jesuits lay low, and then in 1814, Pope Pius VII 'annulled the decrees of his infallible predecessor'[1] and restored the Jesuits to their former position.[2]

---

[1] Hector Macpherson, *The Jesuits in History*, p. 122.
[2] See p. 191.

CHAPTER XVIII

THE CHURCH IN THE STUART PERIOD

THE PURITANS

WHEN James VI of Scotland became James I of England in 1603 the Puritans hoped that, coming from Presbyterian Scotland, he would show them more consideration than had Queen Elizabeth.[1] They did not know his unsatisfactory character. In his early youth, he had learned from his cousin, Esmé Stewart, Duke d'Aubigny, the fatal doctrine of the Divine Right of Kings which was to prove so disastrous to his dynasty. His absolutism could not take kindly to the democratic spirit of Presbyterianism, and his watchword became 'No bishop, no king'. 'Presbytery', he said, 'agrees as well with monarchy as God and the devil.'

The Puritans stood for the Reformed faith as known in Switzerland and France. They objected to the sign of the cross in baptism and to kneeling at the Communion (for fear of adoring the elements). They opposed the use of surplices and albs, and the introduction of certain rites and ceremonies, largely because of their sacerdotal implications. They insisted strongly that everything must be according to the model of the New Testament. They objected to games and sports on the Lord's Day, and their enemies charged them with austerity. In England many of the most learned men of the time were among them, as is seen from the high places they occupied in the universities of Oxford and Cambridge. Their culture is exemplified in the works

[1] See pp. 134 ff.

of Edmund Spenser, Sir Philip Sidney, John Milton and Andrew Marvell, all of whom were Puritans and loved music and poetry. When such men objected to ceremonial and to gorgeous furnishings in churches, they did so, not from lack of aesthetic taste, but on theological grounds. They believed not only that there was beauty in chaste simplicity; they also maintained that this characterized the early Church and that the gradual departure from this simplicity after the third century indicated a spiritual deterioration. They called attention to the prohibition of 'graven images' in the Second Commandment, and urged that the glory of the Deity could never be properly depicted on coloured windows or in sculpture, and that to attempt to do so led to error. They would have agreed heartily with Bernard Lord Manning: 'To call on the name of God, if men truly know and mean what they are doing, is in itself an act so tremendous and so full of comfort that any sensuous or artistic heightening of the effect is not so much a painting of the lily as a varnishing of sunlight.'[1]

While some unreasonable men disparaged music, this was far from being the general attitude. Elaborate church music was objected to because it did not edify the people and because it prevented common folk from joining in the praises of the house of God. While the cultured Puritan stood for simplicity in worship, strictly in accordance with New Testament teaching, he highly valued beauty in other spheres, as may be seen, for example, in the lives of Oliver Cromwell and Colonel Hutchinson.[2] The remarkable strength of the Puritans lay in their constant appeal to Scripture to settle all questions of faith and morals. It was the 'touchstone of God's Word' that counted with them, not the opinions of men. Their earnestness was very

[1] B. L. Manning, *Christian Worship*, p. 163. (Ed. N. Micklem, 1936.)
[2] Cf. Horton Davies, *Worship of the English Puritans*, Appendix B, pp. 268–277.

impressive, and although many mocked them, they increased rapidly in numbers and influence.

At the Hampton Court Conference, called by James I in January 1604, the Puritan leaders were treated with great disrespect by their sovereign. Canon Perry in his *Students' English Church History* says, they were 'insulted, ridiculed, and laughed to scorn without either wit or good manners'. At the end, the king, addressing the learned and courteous Puritan leader, Dr. Reynolds of Oxford, testily declared that he would 'make them conform, or harry them out of the land or worse'. Almost the only good result of this Conference was the production of the Authorized Version of the Bible which was completed in 1611. The king eagerly caught on to a suggestion made by Dr. Reynolds that a new version of the English Bible ought to be made, based on the best Hebrew and Greek texts and compared with earlier translations. It is still in use and the beauty of its English diction, its idiomatic vigour and harmonious rhythm have never been excelled.

When a royal proclamation demanded complete conformity to the settled order of the Church of England on the part of all, and acknowledgment of the king's supremacy, 1,500 clergymen refused to sign the new Canons. Many were shielded by sympathetic bishops, but three hundred ministers in England were ousted and silenced; others were imprisoned. This was the first great rift in the English Church. Bancroft was now archbishop and, as a strong High Churchman, believed in 'the divine right of Prelacy' in the Church. According to Bishop Kennet, he 'proceeded with rigour, severity and wrath' against the Puritans. It was at this time that ornaments and ceremonies which had been discarded for many years were brought back into the Anglican Church.

The next archbishop, Abbot, was more learned and tolerant than Bancroft. He eased the position of Puritans in various ways and secured appointments for some of them in Ireland, to the enrichment of the Irish Church. He influenced King James to authorize the Irish Articles in 1615, thus virtually giving the Puritans in Ireland what was refused them in England, and secured the appointment of Bishop Ussher (the Chronologer) as Primate of the Irish Church. This greatly strengthened evangelicalism in Ireland, and provided a place of refuge for persecuted Puritans, and Covenanters. Abbot also persuaded the king to send deputies to the Calvinistic Synod of Dort in 1618, which gave help and recognition to the Reformed Churches struggling against Romanism on the Continent.

THE PILGRIM FATHERS

Despairing of ever finding liberty of conscience in their own land, a group of men with their wives and families sailed in 1620 from Plymouth to New England in the *Mayflower* to seek liberty in the New World. Because of the theological disturbances caused by their religious views, something must be said about their origin and development.

There had grown up at Scrooby, in Nottinghamshire, a congregation of Independents under the fostering care of William Brewster (in whose home they met), and of John Robinson, who was their pastor. The latter, more than any other, was responsible for organizing and developing the system of church government, first known as 'Independency' and later as 'Congregationalism', because each congregation is autonomous and governed by its own members.

The members of these churches belonged to the separatists from the Church of England who rejected completely the principle of a National Church. In this respect they differed from the Presbyterians. For a long time they were often called Brownists, because Robert Browne had taught their tenets in the reign of Queen Elizabeth. He was imprisoned but escaped in 1582 to Middleburg in Holland, where he formed a congregation, although he soon afterwards re-entered the Anglican Church. In 1583 two pastors in England were put to death because they refused to acknowledge the queen's supremacy in ecclesiastical matters. In 1593 Henry Barrowe and John Greenwood, like Brewster and Robinson graduates of Cambridge, were executed by order of the High Commission Court because of their religious views. Barrowe asserted before the Court that each particular church should govern itself, and he also objected to liturgies. The fate of these good men gives us a glimpse of the intolerance which drove so many Independents into exile.

The members of the Independent church at Scrooby were being similarly sorely harassed by the authorities because of their religious beliefs. As a result they all resolved to emigrate, and in 1608 they settled in Holland. They were unhappy there, however, so, in 1620, they returned to England and then embarked in the *Mayflower* for New England, landing at Plymouth in December. Their sufferings were indescribable in that first winter, and about half of them died. Through faith and indomitable courage, however, the little colony prospered and grew. The tide of Puritan emigration to New England continued and by 1640 twenty thousand had arrived, bent on forming communities where their views of Scripture could find expression. The world then had little idea how much humanity was to owe to the 'Pilgrim Fathers', as they came to be called, and to those other emigrants who founded a great home of liberty in the West.

THE GROWTH OF INDEPENDENCY

Early in the seventeenth century the Baptists emerged as a distinct body. They maintained that baptism ought to be by immersion and that children should not be baptized at all. Only those adults who professed faith in Christ and gave signs of being regenerate should receive this sacrament. In 1611 a group which had separated from an Independent church at Amsterdam came to London under their leader Helwys, and a few years later formed a Baptist church in London. From then onwards their denomination has had continuity. They have often been confused with the Anabaptists, some of whom suffered in England in the sixteenth century.[1] But as early as 1620, when they presented a petition to Parliament, they were recognized by the civil power as being distinct from the Anabaptists. Like the Independents they adopted the congregational form of church government, and took up a separatist attitude to the National Church. This brought on them many sufferings. Under the Commonwealth they enjoyed freedom and flourished, but at the Restoration in 1660 they again had to endure much persecution. An example of this is shown in the twelve years' imprisonment of John Bunyan, one of the greatest Baptists of all time. Soon the denomination began to grow apace in Britain, America and many other lands, and today it numbers some twenty millions.

SOCINUS AND ARMINIUS

These two theologians are of considerable importance because of their effect upon the history of doctrine from the end of the sixteenth century onwards. Faustus Socinus (1539-1604), an Italian, denied the divinity of the Lord Jesus and His atonement for sin. He also rejected the doctrines of original sin and human depravity, and his teachings led to the formation of many 'Unitarian' churches.

Jacobus Arminius (1560-1609), a professor at Leyden, originated the theological system which now bears his name, but it was much developed by his followers who became known as Remonstrants because they presented a Remonstrance to the Estates of Holland against the Calvinistic views held in the Dutch Reformed Church.

[1] See pp. 115 ff.

They affirmed conditional election on the ground of foreseen faith, as against absolute predestination, and declared that the atonement was made for all men, although only believers benefit. They insisted that, while regeneration by the Holy Spirit is necessary, the work of the Holy Spirit can be resisted and rejected, and maintained that the final perseverance of the saints in the way of life is doubtful and that they may relapse from grace and be lost. These views were discussed and condemned by the Synod of Dort which met in 1618, and at which deputies from the English Church were present. Arminianism, however, became the accepted view of the Laudians and the Latitudinarians in the Anglican Church. Later, in the eighteenth century, it became the official doctrine of Methodism, and was also adopted by sections of the Baptist and Congregational Churches. The questions involved are far from being as simple as may appear from a first glance. The Calvinists maintained that, while the Arminian system was attractive to the popular mind, it was lacking in logical consistency.

THE POLICY OF CHARLES I AND ARCHBISHOP LAUD

King Charles and his archbishop stood for the Divine Right of Kings in the State, and the Divine Right of Episcopacy in the Church. The Puritans were 'more than ever discountenanced and persecuted'. Charles was 'so bent on being an absolute, uncontrollable sovereign, that he was resolved to be such a king or none'. He was 'habitually faithless to his pledges'.[1] Laud turned the communion table into an altar, and began the practice of bowing to it. There had been no reference to an 'altar' since the abolition of the sacrifice of the Mass. Parliament manfully sought to defend the Puritans and objected to High Church ceremonies and the erection of altars. When on March 10, 1629, the

[1] Quotations from a letter written by an aristocratic lady who knew King Charles well.

Speaker of the House of Commons, acting on royal instructions, tried to adjourn the House, he was held forcibly in the Chair until Eliot's resolutions against innovations in religion, and against levying taxes without consent of Parliament, were passed. As a result nine members were imprisoned, and for eleven years Charles ruled despotically without a Parliament, Laud being his friend and helper. On the slightest provocation, Puritans were handed over to the Court of High Commission, to suffer crushing fines, life imprisonment, the pillory, or to have their ears cut off or noses slit.

When the famous Long Parliament met in 1640, it refused to vote any money until political and religious grievances were redressed. Fifteen thousand Londoners presented the 'Root and Branch Petition' demanding that Episcopal Church government should be abolished and the faithful preachers should be no longer silenced. It also objected to such practices as bowing to the altar, and the use of images, crucifixes and candles. The king, on receiving from Parliament the Grand Remonstrance which set forth his many acts of misgovernment, went in person to arrest the five members chiefly responsible, but failed. By August 22, 1642, the Civil War had begun.

At first the War went against the Parliamentary party. They were depressed by the early loss of leaders like John Hampden and Lord Brooke. Eventually they appealed to the Scottish people who were already greatly incensed by the king's interference in their own affairs, for help in the fight against royal absolutism.

EVENTS IN SCOTLAND

The Scots had suffered much from Charles' despotic rule. No General Assemblies of the Church had been permitted and the bishops were tools in the hands of Laud who quite misunderstood the Scottish people. When the king and he visited Scotland in 1633 they were amazed at the resistance in Parliament. Laud treated meetings of presbyteries as irregular conventicles and ordered that the new Liturgy and Book of Canons for Scotland should be used by the Presbyterian ministers. Neither the king nor the archbishop would listen to objections.

By the end of 1637, Scotland was in a ferment from end to end. On February 28, 1638, there was signed in Greyfriars Church, Edinburgh, the National Covenant which bound its signatories by an oath to maintain the freedom of the Church. Lords, burghers, and peasants all rallied with enthusiasm to the Presbyterian cause, and copies of the Covenant were signed all over the land. In November, the General Assembly met in Glasgow, the first free Assembly since 1596. The Moderator was Alexander Henderson, a calm, courageous, and wise leader. In spite of peremptory orders from the king to dissolve, they deposed the prelates, abolished the Articles which enslaved the Church, and re-established Presbyterianism. The Episcopal Primate truly declared, 'Our work of thirty years is overthrown at a single stroke.'

King Charles prepared for war, and the Scots put their forces under General Alexander Leslie, and his relative, General David Leslie, superb soldiers who had learnt the art of war under Gustavus Adolphus, the Swedish Protestant king, a truly great military leader. They had notable successes against the king. In 1643 the Scots and the English Parliamentary party entered into the Solemn League and Covenant binding themselves to seek the reformation of religion according to the example of the best Reformed Churches—what many excellent men had long sought for, although overborne by royal autocracy. The Westminister Assembly of Divines met from July 1, 1643, until February 22, 1649, with the object of finding a basis for a united Church for the whole of Britain. Its members were mostly outstanding graduates of Oxford and Cambridge; scholars whose piety and learning would have graced any gathering, and the few Scottish representatives were in no way inferior to the rest. These men gave the clearest and most orderly presentation of divine truth ever set forth in a Confession of Faith. The Westminster Confession was adopted in Scotland in 1647, and has remained the symbol of Presbyterian churches throughout the English-speaking world. It is the finest fruit of Reformed theology.

The bloody battles of the great Civil War were fought between 1642 and 1646, the Scots fighting with the English parliamentary forces against the royalist party. In time, Cromwell, in his 'New Model' army, forged an instrument by which the parliamentary party gained a crushing victory. The Independents and sectaries, who figured so prominently in Cromwell's forces, were determined to bring the king to execution. The Presbyterians did not wish to go to this extreme, and were therefore 'purged' from the House of Commons by the military dictatorship. Charles I was condemned to death, and beheaded at Whitehall on January 30, 1649.

THE RESTORATION

The Scottish leaders had Charles II crowned at Scone. He went hypocritically through the mockery of swearing to support the Solemn League and Covenant, although his sympathies were Roman Catholic. Loyalty to an unworthy dynasty led the Scots to fight and die for an unprincipled profligate, and to break with Oliver Cromwell, one of the greatest Englishmen of all time, with whom they had much in common.

The great ideal of religious liberty cherished by Cromwell was wrecked through the wild intransigence of many of the sectaries who surrounded him. On his death in 1658, the Presbyterians, then very numerous in England, took a leading part in bringing back Charles II. They met, however, with nothing but hostility from the new régime. Because of the Act of

Uniformity of 1662, which demanded complete acceptance of the Anglican Prayer-Book in every jot and tittle, no less than 2,000 Presbyterian, Independent and Baptist ministers heroically resigned their livings. The Corporation Act (1661), the Five Mile Act (1665), and the Test Act (1673), placed under further serious disability every Englishman who was not an Anglican Churchman.

Charles II made a secret treaty with Louis XIV that, when the time should be opportune, he would declare himself openly a Roman Catholic. Then, with Louis' help, he would establish absolute government and the Roman Catholic faith in Britain. The policy of his Parliament, however, was unbending. There was to be no concession of any kind to either Roman Catholics or Nonconformists. As a result there was much suffering for conscience' sake. For example, John Bunyan, a Baptist, was imprisoned for twelve years in Bedford jail and there wrote *The Pilgrim's Progress,* now recognized as one of the world's greatest religious books. Of a somewhat different type was George Fox who, in the same period, founded the Society of Friends, known as the Quakers. He, too, suffered much for his convictions. During these years of persecution many emigrated to North America. Among them was the young aristocrat, William Penn, who introduced Quakerism into the colony of Pennsylvania, which he founded in 1682, and so gave the Society of Friends a notable place in the New World.

The unbelievable folly of the Scottish people in espousing the cause of Charles II brought untold suffering to the land. The 'Drunken Parliament' in Edinburgh carried out the behests of Charles and once more imposed Episcopacy upon the Church. There followed the disastrous defeats of the Covenanters at Bothwell Bridge and Rullion Green. Then the staunchest Presbyterians organized their Societies, and when forbidden to worship God in public, met in secret amid the moorland mists and the deep ravines of the southern uplands of Scotland—constantly hunted down by men like Graham of Claverhouse and Grierson of Lag with their dragoons. No less than 17,000 suffered in one way or other for conscience' sake during their heroic Covenanting struggle; many being executed at the Mercat Cross and in the Grass Market of Edinburgh.

Under James II, who was an avowed Roman Catholic, the doings of the atrocious Judge Jeffreys in England filled people in every denomination with horror. Now, not only Scottish Covenanters, but English bishops refused to bend the knee before Stuart tyranny. Before the popular uprising, James II fled, and, in 1688, William of Orange and Mary were invited to occupy the throne.

It was the beginning of a new epoch and made for lasting stability in Church and State. In England, the Anglican Church was approved as the established Church. The Toleration Act of 1689 alleviated the position of Nonconformists but inequalities continued for many years. In a short period they grew up so rapidly in numbers that one thousand new places of worship were built. By this time, three parties were distinguishable in the Anglican Church—High, Evangelical, and Broad (or Latitudinarian).

In Scotland, the Revolution Settlement of 1689-1690 brought great joy to an overwhelming majority of the people. The Presbyterian Church was once again established, and the sovereign came under obligations to recognize it. The Westminster Confession of Faith was taken as expressing the creed of the Scottish Church, and these measures were solemnly recognized by statute. It was a day of wonderful deliverance after all the horrors of the 'Killing Times'.

SUMMARY OF EVENTS IN EUROPE

On the Continent during the first half of the seventeenth century the feud between Protestants and

Roman Catholics culminated in the Thirty Years' War (1618-1648). The intervention of Gustavus Adolphus, the Christian King of Sweden, whose territories were then very extensive, mightily helped the flagging Protestants. Many parts of Germany were devastated in this great conflict, which was ended by the Peace of Westphalia in 1648. Protestantism was then given a recognition on the Continent such as it had never received before; the Lutheran and Calvinistic forms of it being equally recognized. Formerly, Calvinism had been scarcely tolerated by the Empire.

In France, Louis XIV, in order to further his own autocratic aims, supported in 1682 the claim of the French Catholics to enjoy 'the Gallican Liberties', and to be free from the intervention of the pope in the temporal concerns of the nations. They claimed a certain freedom from the Vatican, even in ecclesiastical affairs. But there was no liberty for Protestants. The king's tyrannical policy led in 1685 to the revocation of the Edict of Nantes.[1] Under this cruel blow, 400,000 Huguenots fled from their country and greatly enriched other lands, including Britain, with their industry, skill and great human worth.

[1] See p. 124.

CHAPTER XIX

THE EIGHTEENTH CENTURY

A PERIOD OF DECAY

THIS century does not stand high spiritually and yet during it there arose evangelical movements of vast importance. Wearied to death by the wars and struggles of the previous century, men were now glad to 'sit at ease in Zion',[1] and this inactivity bred stagnation in the Church. The religious outlook of the period was profoundly affected by the rise of Deism. This system of thought originated in England and was the outcome of those philosophical and scientific ideas which had come into prominence in the seventeenth century. Men like Lord Bacon, Hobbes, Descartes, Kepler, Galileo, and Isaac Newton, based their scientific conclusions on reason and the inductive method. Observation and experiment suggested that the universe was ruled by natural law. The belief then became common that this law was immutable. Hence, God began to be regarded by some thinkers as an absentee deity who had set the universe in motion and then had left it to itself under inflexible natural laws. Thus there was no place for the supernatural in this world. The incarnation, miracles, prophecy and the divine inspiration of the Scriptures were ruled out as being doctrines no longer worthy of belief.

Among the leading exponents of these Deistic views were John Toland, who in 1696 published *Christianity not Mysterious*; and Matthew Tindal, the author of *Christianity as Old as Creation*, written in 1730. From

[1] Amos vi. 1.

England, Deism spread to Germany and France. In the former country it took shape as 'The Enlightenment' associated with Christian Wolff and Kant in philosophy, and with Goethe and Lessing in literature. In France it profoundly influenced the Encyclopaedists who were a group of brilliant scientific and literary men who contributed articles to the *Encyclopaedia*. Among them were outstanding Roman Catholic clergymen. By following out their principle that everything was dominated by an inflexible natural law they raised doubts among Churchmen as to the Christian doctrines which depended on divine revelation. For them, reason was the final arbiter, not revelation. David Hume's *Treatise of Human Nature* (1739) and Voltaire's works, somewhat later, were features of the period. These strong tendencies to unbelief had their natural culmination in the French Revolution in 1789. In the Continental Universities, Deism developed into Rationalism, and then returned with renewed force to British centres of learning.

In Germany, the Pietists, who largely owed their evangelical outlook to the writings of John Bunyan and Richard Baxter, had exercised no small influence on religious life through the Universities from about 1670. This was largely due to Philip Spener (1635-1705), and August Hermann Francke (1663-1727) who, at the University of Halle, stressed the evil of sin and the need for atonement in much the same way as did the English Puritans. Their influence spread, and among those affected was Count Zinzendorf who allowed a group of Moravian Brethren (a branch of the Church of John Hus) to settle on his estate at Herrnhut in Saxony in 1722. This small group became the pioneers of modern missionary enterprise and profoundly influenced the thinking of churchmen in various lands. Unfortunately, the spread of the warmhearted faith of the Pietists was arrested by the rise of Rationalism, and the development of Deism; and, in the German Church as a whole, the cold critical teachings of the philosophy of Wolff prevailed.

Semler (1725-1791) and Eichhorn (1752-1827) marked a new era in the criticism of the Bible. They rejected its divine inspiration and refused to believe in miracles and prophecy. While Christ was exalted as a Teacher, the New Testament doctrine of salvation through His atoning death was not accepted.[1] The result was the spread of unbelief until men like Tholuck, Dorner, and Delitzsch brought about a revival of Reformation doctrine in the following century.

In England the evil trend was seen in the growing influence of Latitudinarianism in the Anglican Church, and Unitarianism among Presbyterians and General Baptists. The full deity of our Lord was widely denied and spiritual deadness invaded congregations. In Scotland, the 'Moderates' were in the ascendant and decried fervent evangelical preaching and all enthusiasm in religion. True, certain apologists like Bishop Butler, Bishop Berkeley, and Waterland, had done excellent work early in the century, but it made little impression on the mass of the people. The words of Mark Pattison were substantially true: it was a period of 'decay in religion, licentiousness of morals, public corruption, and profaneness of language'.[2]

THE EVANGELICAL REVIVAL

It was at such a time as this that a wonderful awakening from God came to the whole of Great Britain. In Wales it began largely as the result of the faithful ministry of men such as Griffith Jones, Daniel Rowlands, and Howell Harris. In England it is closely linked with the names of John and Charles Wesley and George Whitefield. In 1729, the Wesleys with some other student friends founded at Oxford 'The Holy

[1] John Cairns, *Unbelief in the 18th Century*, pp. 190–191.
[2] Mark Pattison, *Essays*, II, p. 42.

Club', their aim being to promote in themselves and others the more faithful observance of the Christian religion. In derision their fellow students gave them the name 'Methodists'. Few of the members of the Club, however, had then a personal experience of conversion and forgiveness of sin.

George Whitefield

It was not until 1735 that Whitefield, overwhelmed by the dreadful burden of his sins, found what he called 'inexpressible peace' through a living faith in Christ. His first sermon, preached at Gloucester on June 27, 1736, was so unusual in its treatment of sin that many were scandalized. But there were fifteen conversions. His next sermon was on the 'new birth', from the text 'If any man be in Christ, he is a new creature' (2 Cor. v. 17). He roundly rejected the doctrine of baptismal regeneration, then widely received in the Anglican Church, and stressed the absolute necessity of being regenerated by the Holy Spirit in accordance with the teaching of Christ.[1] He denied that one who never fights against the world, the flesh, and the devil, can be a real Christian simply because a few drops of water had been sprinkled on him. For him the new birth was a mighty spiritual change, wrought in the penitent by the Spirit of God, and one which transformed the heart. This teaching caused strong opposition. Shut out from many pulpits, and severely censured in the newspapers, he yet drew immense crowds and many professed conversion. He preached to vast gatherings of miners in the open air—men who were alienated from the organized churches—and the Spirit of God worked mightily among them. Thousands of them became earnest followers of Christ.

When Whitefield visited America for the first time in 1738, he became a life-long friend of Jonathan Edwards, under whom, four years earlier, a mighty

[1] See Jn. iii. 3–11.

revival had taken place in New England. During his long ministry he returned frequently to North America and exerted a profound spiritual influence upon the new colonies there.

John Wesley

In spite of his enthusiasm and incessant activity as a member of the 'Holy Club' at Oxford, John Wesley also was without any personal assurance of salvation, and when he went as a missionary to Georgia in 1736 his work was a failure. On the voyage out, however, and in Georgia itself, he made contact with members of the Moravian Brethren, contacts which were momentous for himself and for the whole English-speaking world. He realized that they had a faith in Christ as their personal Saviour which he did not possess. He saw that this made their whole being radiate with a great joy. On his return to London in 1738 they made him realize the meaning of the saving change wrought by the new birth. After a great mental struggle during which he passed through times of darkness and terrible depression, he finally came into the light on May 24, 1738, at a meeting of an evangelical society in Aldersgate, London. Wesley wrote in his Journal: 'I felt my heart strangely warmed. I felt I did trust in Christ, Christ alone, for salvation; and an assurance was given me, that He had taken away *my* sins, even *mine*, and saved me from the law of sin and death.'

After his conversion, Wesley embarked on that great work of evangelism with which his name will ever be associated. Because of his preaching on man's lost condition through sin, regeneration through the Holy Spirit, and salvation through the cleansing power of Christ's blood, he found, like Whitefield, that many pulpits were closed to him. There was much ecclesiastical opposition, as well as the opposition of ungodly mobs. Nothing, however, could stop this dauntless herald of the cross. In fifty years he travelled 250,000 miles, mostly on horseback, during his evangelistic tours. Remarkable scenes were constantly witnessed as he preached the gospel. Hardened sinners could be seen at open-air meetings with tears of penitence rolling down their cheeks. The roughest in the land came humbly to the foot of the cross. Wesley was an Arminian[1] in theology, but was loved by most Calvinists because of his passionate proclamation of salvation to sinners. The Methodist Church, which he founded, has today thirty million communicant members throughout the world, beside a vast number of adherents.

George Whitefield did not himself found a denomination. He was greatly helped by the pious and wealthy Countess of Huntingdon. The Anglican Church received no small evangelical impetus through his work. In Wales, his followers founded the Calvinistic Methodist Church, now known as the Presbyterian Church of Wales. Just as God had touched the hearts of men like Griffith Jones, Howell Harris and Daniel Rowlands, and used them mightily in Wales before the great awakening in England began under Wesley and Whitefield, so now in the Church of England the Spirit of God raised up ministers of virile evangelical faith, who had been affected only indirectly by the revival movements under Wesley and Whitefield. This movement in the Church of England was largely Calvinistic. The result, however, of all the movements was a wonderful strengthening of Evangelicalism throughout the land. To this day the heart of many a Christian warms at the mention of such names as Fletcher of Madeley, Samuel Walker of Truro, William Grimshaw of Haworth, John Berridge of Everton, William Romaine of London and Augustus Toplady, author of *Rock of Ages*. Such men were greatly blessed to their

[1]See pp. 155 f.

own generation and handed on in the National Church a great tradition of evangelistic zeal.

Charles Simeon

Of all the English Church Evangelicals of that period, however, Charles Simeon of Cambridge made the profoundest and most lasting impression. Coming up to King's College in 1779, he found Cambridge almost moribund as far as religion was concerned in spite of its great spiritual traditions inherited from Reformation times. A young man of intense sincerity, Simeon soon awakened to the need of putting himself right with God, and made the momentous discovery, in his own words, that he could transfer his guilt to another. 'I sought', he wrote, 'to lay my sins on the sacred head of Jesus.' There were few at the University then who held his point of view, for the great evangelical revival had scarcely touched Cambridge. Ordained to the ministry in 1782, he became vicar of Holy Trinity at the age of twenty-three. He was already a Fellow of his college.

Almost at once his church became thronged with worshippers. At first, however, he had many opponents, including the majority of his parishioners, for his presentation of the gospel was something new to Cambridge at that period, and seemed unbalanced and too enthusiastic. Gradually he found staunch friends among outstanding members of the University, and in spite of continued hostility, his influence increased apace. His saintly life and his sane scholarship made an abiding impression upon a vast number of students.

Few men have ever done a more remarkable work in guiding the footsteps of suitable men towards the office of the Christian ministry. But it was not just the Church in the homeland in which he was interested. He did immense service in promoting foreign missionary enterprise and through him many devoted their lives to the evangelization of the heathen, outstanding among them being the young Cambridge scholar, Henry Martyn. Simeon was remarkably effective both in preaching and teaching the great truths of the Christian faith, and when he died in 1836, all Cambridge mourned his loss and recognized that a great man had gone from their midst.

Events in Scotland

In Scotland the dead hand of Moderatism had a serious effect upon the Church. In 1733, Ebenezer Erskine, and three others were driven from the Church of Scotland because of their opposition to the Patronage Act of 1712, under which patrons could nominate ministers contrary to the will of the people. Their vigorous evangelicalism could not tolerate such a situation and they founded the Secession Church. In 1752 Thomas Gillespie was shamefully treated for similar causes and he founded the Relief Church. These churches flourished in the towns and burghs of Scotland and by the end of the century had five hundred places of worship. Their testimony was most valuable in those days of spiritual deadness. The main part of these two bodies united later to form the United Presbyterian Church.

In 1740 occurred the great Revival of Cambuslang, near Glasgow. After the movement had begun under the minister, Mr. William MacCulloch of the Church of Scotland, they received a visit from George Whitefield, who one Sunday preached in the open air to 40,000 people. Unprecedented scenes were witnessed and the effects were widespread. A young minister who was influenced then, nobly led the Evangelicals within the Church of Scotland for 60 years. He was Dr. John Erskine of Greyfriars Church, Edinburgh. Moderatism, however, continued in the ascendant until well into the next century.

During the first half of the eighteenth century there were three Jacobite risings in the Scottish Highlands (1715, 1719, and 1745) all aimed at bringing back the

Stuart dynasty to the British throne. They had no small sympathy, and even some help from English Jacobites. The defeat of these rebellions definitely settled that the British monarchy must be Protestant and made for peace and stability. The romance and heroism of these movements have blinded the eyes of many to their real meaning.

The latter part of the century saw the revolt of the American Colonies, and the founding of the United States. Independence greatly affected the development of every phase of life in America, including the ecclesiastical. One great change was the establishment of the principle that all religions should enjoy complete liberty, and that there should be no State Church. In 1789 came the French Revolution with all its violence and bloodshed culminating, in 1793, in the Reign of Terror when the 'goddess of reason' was set up in Paris on the altar of Notre Dame, and the wild cry went up, 'There is no God.' The Roman Church was identified by the people with the earlier misgovernment of France and suffered greatly. At the end of the century Napoleon appeared. He led the French army which entered Rome in 1796, and compelled the pontiff to cede one-third of the papal territories. In 1799 when the pope raised difficulties he was removed to France after Napoleon had turned Rome into a republic. The latter, however, was very conscious of the value of an alliance with the Roman Catholic Church from a political and social point of view. Hence he entered into a Concordat with the papacy in 1801. Under it, all bishops had to resign and new ones were nominated by Napoleon.[1]

Altogether the century was a difficult one for the Roman Catholic Church, but in Britain a more generous and tolerant attitude was gradually being manifested. Thus, in 1737, some of the disabilities of

[1] See p. 190.

Irish Roman Catholics were removed. In 1780 the government permitted Roman Catholics to hold land once more in England. The sympathy shown to sufferers in the French Revolution produced good feeling among English Catholics, and all this paved the way for the Catholic Emancipation Act of 1829.

The eighteenth century was marked in England by a great outburst of sacred song. While Addison and Bishop Ken had written hymns which found wide acceptance, it was Isaac Watts (1674-1748) who first made the period notable for its hymnology. He began by writing paraphrases of the Psalms which have left an indelible impression, such as 'Jesus shall reign where'er the sun' (on the 72nd Psalm); and 'O God, our help in ages past' (on the 90th). Then he proceeded to write hymns which have found a lasting place in the churches. Among these are 'Come, let us join our cheerful songs'; 'I'm not ashamed to own my Lord'; and 'Come, ye that love the Lord'. He did more than any other man to break down in the Dissenting Churches the Puritan tradition of using the Psalms only in singing God's praise in public worship. There are some who regret this aspect of his work.

Philip Doddridge (1702-1751), the great Dissenting divine, who wrote *The Rise and Progress of Religion in the Soul*, was also the author of many hymns. Among the best known of these are 'Hark, the glad sound, the Saviour comes' and 'O happy day that fixed my choice'. Then there were the *Olney Hymns* published by John Newton (1725-1807), the well-beloved curate of Olney in Buckinghamshire and later rector of St. Mary Woolnoth in London. Many of these hymns are still widely used. For example, 'How sweet the name of Jesus sounds' comes from this collection. His friend, the poet Cowper, contributed sixty-eight hymns to the book, and many of these have become equally well-known. It was, however, Charles Wesley (1708-1788), the brother of

John Wesley, who produced the greatest number of hymns in that period. Like his brother he was a preacher; but his fame now rests on his hymns rather than on his sermons. John S. Simon wrote: 'Charles Wesley's hymns convey clear and decisive teaching on the subjects of sin, righteousness, and judgment. The exceeding sinfulness of sin is set forth in uncompromising language; and the perfect righteousness of Jesus is displayed.'[1] A large number of his hymns are now found in nearly every collection.

[1] John S. Simon, *Revival of Religion in the Eighteenth Century*, p. 303.

CHAPTER XX

MODERN MISSIONARY EXPANSION

NOTHING can be more remarkable than the difference between the intense missionary zeal of the Church in the early centuries and the slowness of the Church in the modern epoch to awaken to its responsibilities in this respect. True, the Jesuits and other Roman Catholic Orders began a remarkable work in the second quarter of the sixteenth century in India, the East Indies, and Japan, a project later extended to China and other lands. It was, however, a work which was largely concerned with externals. All that seems to have been required of the 'converts' was that they should observe a few ceremonies, and be able to repeat the Lord's Prayer along with the Creed and to cross their arms over their breasts.[1] The French occupation of vast territories in North America, and the Spanish and Portuguese conquests throughout Central and South America opened to the Roman Church a field so great as to be difficult to visualize. While individual priests and monks showed wonderful devotion and heroism, no one would seriously claim that the Roman Church showed itself full of spiritual vitality during the three hundred and fifty years when it was virtually the only representative of Christianity from the Rio Grande down to Tierra del Fuego. It is, however, a remarkable fact that in North America, where it existed side by side with Protestantism, Roman Catholicism developed a zeal and energy greatly in ex-

[1] Hector MacPherson, *The Jesuits in History*, p. 34.

cess of anything which existed in the South, where that religion had a free field.

The first British missionary endeavours are connected with efforts to convert the Red Indians in the new American colonies. Under Cromwell, Parliament formed in 1649 'the Corporation for the Propagation of the Gospel in New England', with which are associated the self-sacrificing labours of John Eliot (1604-1690), and the Mayhew family, which strove for generations for the conversion of the American Indians. Then, later, we have John Sergeant and David Brainerd, the friend of Jonathan Edwards, who, although he died within three years of commencing the work, did much to arouse the Church to the needs of the Indians. All these were friends of Whitefield who, himself, through the effect of his teaching upon John Newton, Claudius Buchanan, William Wilberforce, and Thomas Scott, liberated immense missionary energies which began to manifest themselves soon after his death.

In the sixteenth and seventeenth centuries, as the Dutch extended their colonies in Malaya, India, Ceylon and other places, their missionaries did a noble work, especially when Pietism began to enter Holland through contacts with the English Puritans. The German Pietists, with their evangelical fervour, had a marked effect upon the development of Missions through the teaching of August Herman Franke (1663-1727) of Halle University. The Lutheran Church had fallen upon a period of formality and spiritual deadness, but Pietism brought a new life to many. In co-operation with the king of Denmark's chaplain, Franke organized the Danish-Halle Mission to India in 1705, when Ziegenbalg and Plutschau, the first Protestant missionaries to India, began a truly notable work in Tranquebar, where they translated the whole New Testament into the Tamil language, and set up a printing press. Their most bitter enemies were often European officials of the trading companies from the

Protestant lands of Britain, Holland, and Denmark.

The next landmark in the history of Protestant Missions is the work of the Moravian 'Unitas Fratrum'. In spite of almost ceaseless persecution, the followers of John Hus (martyred in 1415) lived on, often in 'caves and dens of the earth'. In 1722 a group of them fled from Austrian intolerance in Moravia, and settled on the estates of Count Zinzendorf of Herrnhut in Silesian Saxony. He had been profoundly moved by the Pietist teaching of Spener and Franke. He and his wife early covenanted with God to give their wealth for the proclamation of the gospel among the heathen. On their land was organized the Moravian Missionary Church in 1732. The achievements of this small, Spirit-filled Church, which was run on lines of apostolic simplicity and faith, fill us with wonder. There were less than 600 people in Herrnhut at the beginning, yet in twenty-five years they sent out eighteen missionaries to different parts of the world. In one hundred and fifty years they sent out no less than 2,170 missionaries. But even more important was the spiritual influence they exerted in many lands, as in the conversion of John Wesley and other great Christian leaders, which in turn reacted most powerfully on the development of modern missions. Yet for over sixty years the great Churches of Europe, infected with Deism, Rationalism and a dead formality, looked coldly on while this mighty work of God developed.

The East India Company, which was the forerunner of the British Empire in India, professed, in its earlier days, much interest in the religious welfare of its employees, and of the natives. Chaplains were appointed in many centres and, although these were not expressly missionaries, they helped to evangelize some of the Indian people. Before the end of the eighteenth century, however, the Company had become a bitter enemy of Christian missions, so much so that they would not allow William Carey, the first English foreign missionary of modern times, to enter their territory, and he had to settle in Serampore, which was under the Danes.

William Carey (1761-1834) stands out as one of the greatest missionaries since apostolic days. Born in Northamptonshire, he became a cobbler, but showed a remarkable genius for natural science and for languages. Falling under the powerful evangelical influence of men like Thomas Scott and Andrew Fuller, he became a Baptist minister. He strongly advocated the sending of missions to the heathen, and gave his ministerial brethren no peace. At one meeting, an old minister told him sternly, 'Sit down, young man, and respect the opinions of your seniors. If the Lord wants to convert the heathen, He can do it without your help.' His persistence led to the founding of the Baptist Missionary Society in 1792 at Kettering, with Andrew Fuller as Secretary. That day twelve poor Baptist ministers subscribed £13 2s. 6d.—a large sum for them. It was the beginning of a mighty work for the kingdom of God. Next year Carey set out for India. A few years later he was joined by Marshman and Ward who were equally enthusiastic. They supported themselves by teaching. Carey pointed the way for succeeding missionaries in India, and within half a century of his death in 1834 there were half a million Protestants among the natives of that land.

As stirring reports of William Carey's work in Bengal began to reach home, Presbyterians, Anglicans and Congregationalists were aroused to form a Missionary Society for non-Baptists, and the famous London Missionary Society was founded in 1795. In this, and in all the missionary societies formed about the end of the eighteenth century, may be seen the fruits of the great evangelical awakening which had been going on for about fifty years. While the denominations as such were still apathetic to the clamant call for the evangelization of the heathen, good men whose souls the Lord had touched formed these independent missionary-sending agencies.

Stirred by the story of Captain's Cook's *Voyages* in the South Pacific, the London Missionary Society in 1796 sent thirty missionaries to that region. Its vigorous work spread to India, China, Africa, Madagascar, and the West Indies. Its famous missionaries included Robert Morrison (1782-1834) pioneer missionary to China, John Williams (1796-1839) of the South Pacific, martyred on Eromanga Island, Robert and Mary Moffat, and their renowned son-in-law, David Livingstone, the African missionary and explorer, and James Chalmers, a native of Argyll, who did a great work on Rarotonga and New Guinea where he was slain by cannibals.

What was known as *The Clapham Sect* furnishes us with a remarkable example of the deep spiritual devotion, missionary zeal, and practical Christianity of Anglican Church Evangelicals towards the end of the eighteenth century. Its members belonged mostly to the upper classes. They began to meet together for prayer and Bible study because of the grave situation which presented itself at the time of the French Revolution, and held their meetings in Clapham, in the neighbourhood of which most of them lived. The widespread nature of their activities and the success which attended them is astonishing.

It was largely through their help and their enthusiasm that the agitation for the abolition of the slave-trade was successful. Zachary Macaulay had seen the evils of it while managing an estate in Jamaica. From 1787 onwards they kept the matter before Parliament. William Wilberforce took up the question with untiring energy and finally persuaded William Pitt to promote a Bill for the total abolition of the slave trade in

1807. In 1833 all slaves in British territory were emancipated. Members of the group, with the object of showing how the negroes ought to be treated, had already founded the Colony of Sierra Leone of which Zachary Macaulay was governor for seven years.

These Christians at Clapham also demonstrated how effective an instrument Christian literature could be in disseminating ideas of the right kind. Wilberforce founded the *Christian Observer* in 1801 and exposed the evils of slavery. James Stephen followed along the same lines. The vigorous pamphlets of Hannah More on such subjects as *Village Politics* led to the founding of the Religious Tract Society, which has done a work of priceless value throughout the years. Encouraged by Wilberforce she was instrumental in founding schools in Somerset, and other members of the Society also did much for the promotion of education.

Charles Grant, a rich East India merchant, wrote a pamphlet in 1792 calling for the toleration of Christian Missions by the East India Company. He helped forward the building of churches in India and played a leading part in promoting missionary effort in various lands. Other members of this group took an important share in founding the British and Foreign Bible Society of which John Thornton, a banker and merchant, in whose house at Clapham the members often met, was the first Treasurer. Five years later the National Bible Society of Scotland was founded, and the American Bible Society came into existence about the same time. The importance of these Societies for Christian work at home and abroad cannot be exaggerated.

These Christian leaders also realized the importance of maintaining the Lord's Day as a sacred heritage, and William Wilberforce founded a Society for its defence. In addition he and his friends were foremost in promoting schemes for social betterment throughout the land and in this respect favourably influenced the legislature. In the purely spiritual field, a notable step forward was taken in establishing the Islington Clerical Conference, an annual gathering of evangelical Anglican clergy which still continues. But, apart from the abolition of slavery, the most outstanding achievement of the Clapham Sect was the part taken by its members, along with others, in forming in 1799 the Church Missionary Society, now the largest Society of its kind in the British Commonwealth. It was the outcome of the great evangelical movement then stirring the Church of England. In addition to members of the group such as Wilberforce and Charles Grant, men like Charles Simeon of Cambridge, whose missionary zeal we have already noted, and Thomas Scott, the Bible commentator, were connected with its foundation. The Society spread to India, West Africa, the Niger, Victoria Nyanza, Egypt, Palestine, Persia, China and Japan. Among the outstanding men who served this Society was Henry Martyn, a Senior Wrangler, who has been described as Cambridge's greatest missionary, and whose memory is perpetuated by the Henry Martyn Hall in that city. He took up missionary work in Calcutta in 1806, and in a short time translated the New Testament and the English Church Prayer-Book into Hindustani. In connection with further plans for translation work he removed to Persia where he died at the early age of thirty-one, having made only one direct convert. The touching example of self-sacrifice given by this brilliant student, who was cut off before his work had well begun, stimulated many others to offer themselves for missionary service.

The General Methodist Society was founded in 1796. Its labours extended to the West Indies, South Africa, South India, China, Polynesia and other lands. In the same year two Missionary Societies were formed in Scotland by individual ministers and laymen of the Church of Scotland and the Secession Church. Chief among them was Dr. John Erskine of Greyfriars

Church, Edinburgh. Still under Moderate dominance, the Church of Scotland was then officially opposed to Foreign Missions. These Societies did magnificent work in Sierra Leone, India, Jamaica and South Africa, and were later taken over by the Scottish Churches. Among the great missionaries was Alexander Duff of India— the first missionary ever sent out by a church as distinct from a society. This was in 1829.

The China Inland Mission, founded in 1866 by Dr. Hudson Taylor, has been wonderfully blessed. Thousands of devoted men and women have laboured for this great interdenominational society. It is typical of the large number of so-called 'Faith Missions', many of which have contributed in an outstanding way to the building up of the kingdom of God overseas. Unfortunately our space will not allow an examination of their history. Nor is there room to describe in detail the vast work done by the American missionary organizations in the nineteenth and twentieth centuries. The contribution which they have made to the task of world evangelism is of the highest importance. Without the generous giving of the American churches and the devoted service of American missionaries the expansion of effort seen in more recent years would have been quite impossible.

The great missionary work of the various denominational and interdenominational societies now encircles the globe. From their labours have arisen young and vigorous churches which are fast taking an important place beside the older denominations. The nineteenth century was pre-eminently the century of missionary expansion. The Churches were difficult to arouse to their responsibility for the heathen, but once the work really began it extended and flourished to an unexampled degree.

CHAPTER XXI

THE NINETEENTH CENTURY

THE nineteenth century was a great century in human history, and its astonishing social, economic, and scientific progress was closely linked with the religious life of the period. The evangelical movement which began in the previous century grew and developed in a remarkable way. This is true not only of the Dissenting Churches but also of the Anglican Church, where the evangelical section became a powerful influence in the life of the country during the first half of the nineteenth century. The same can be said of the evangelical forces in America and Scotland.

In the Anglican Church we have already noted the great work done at Cambridge by Charles Simeon in inspiring young men to dedicate themselves to the service of Christ at home and overseas,[1] and the multifarious activities of the Clapham Sect[2] associated with the names of such Christian leaders as Henry Thornton, William Wilberforce and Zachary Macaulay. There was also the far-reaching influence of Thomas Scott, who made the Bible live through his commentary and other writings, and who did much to arouse interest in Missions.

The same spiritual vitality is seen among Nonconformists in such movements as the emancipation of the slaves in which T. J. Buxton and John Smith of Demerara distinguished themselves, the founding of

[1] See pp. 169 f.　　[2] See pp. 178 ff.

Sunday Schools in 1783 by Robert Raikes with the object of teaching children to read the Bible, and prison reform, which is for ever associated with the names of John Howard and Elizabeth Fry. Trevelyan reckons that 'the Nonconformists rose from about one-twentieth of the church-goers to something near a half' during this period.

The Industrial Revolution was raising many problems, and Christian statesmen, such as the great Lord Shaftesbury, were zealous in promoting Bills to ameliorate the hard lot of factory workers, especially women and young children, to stop the opium trade, to protect the Lord's Day, and to put an end to flogging in the army.[1] All such movements were symptomatic of the new life which had come to the churches through the Evangelical Revival. Increasing stress was laid on the need for education. In England Christian statesmen could see the dangers of illiteracy, especially in the rapidly expanding urban areas. But it was felt strongly that all schools should have a religious foundation and should not be under the secular control of the State. The Anglicans founded the National Society in 1811 and this was followed by the Nonconformist British and Foreign School Society in 1814. In later years, there was from time to time much rivalry between these bodies. But both were motivated by a desire to relieve the ignorance and misery of the poorer classes, and it is on the foundation which they laid that later State education was built. In Scotland, thanks to the stress laid by the Reformer, John Knox, on his great ideal 'a Church and a school in every parish', there was, by the beginning of the century, a remarkable number of schools already in existence.

THE CHRISTIAN BRETHREN

In 1827 originated the religious body known as the

[1] See the section dealing with the activities of the 'Clapham Sect', pp. 178 ff.

Christian Brethren. It was destined to exercise a considerable influence upon the spiritual life of Britain and America. It began in Dublin and soon passed to England. Among its early leaders were Anthony Norris Groves, a returned missionary, J. G. Bellett, a lawyer, W. F. Hutchinson of Dublin, John V. Parnell, afterwards Lord Congleton, and Dr. Cronin. They were joined by John Nelson Darby, a Londoner then serving as an Anglican curate in Ireland. He was not only possessed of considerable intellectual gifts, but led a consecrated life and became the most outstanding leader among the Brethren. In its early days the movement was supported largely by people of the upper middle class, but in due time it began to reach the working classes also. Anthony Norris Groves declared, 'Our aim is that men should come together in all simplicity as disciples, not waiting on any pulpit or ministry, but trusting that the Lord will edify us together by ministering to us, as He sees good, from ourselves.' This indicates what has been their purpose ever since. They dreaded clericalism and stressed that their assemblies must be led by the Holy Spirit, and that all true Christians were priests. To them, many of the churches seemed to be worldly and dead, whilst others were orthodox but too cold. They also gave a prominent place in their preaching to the doctrine of Christ's Second Coming, a subject which had been popularized at that time by Edward Irving, the far-famed and eloquent minister of the Church of Scotland in Regent Square, London.

At Plymouth the movement became strong under the leadership of B. W. Newton. There the name 'Plymouth Brethren' had its origin. In 1847 Newton was accused of heresy. Having withdrawn, he set up another meeting place in Plymouth and ultimately became an independent minister in London. In Bethesda Chapel, Bristol, George Müller, the well-known founder of the Homes for orphan children, and Henry Craik, were

joint pastors. They took up a position similar to that
of the Brethren, and were joined by some of Newton's
followers who had come from Plymouth. This was condemned by Darby who represented the 'Exclusive' type
of Brethrenism, while Müller and Craik became leaders
of the 'Open' section which was prepared to co-operate
and have fellowship with Christians from outside their
own religious body. The Exclusive Brethren have had,
at times, considerable divisions among themselves over
doctrinal questions, and it has not been possible to
bring about a fusion with the Open section which has
shown a spirit of fraternity towards other communions.
Darby died in 1882 and Müller in 1898.

The Brethren today are a living force with a simple
faith based upon an infallible Bible. They teach that
men are lost through sin and can be saved from divine
judgment only by faith in Jesus Christ. Because of the
surpassing importance of the life hereafter, the salvation of the soul is for them far more important than
social reform or political philosophy. They are well
represented in the universities and in business life,
and their members carry on a quiet but effective
work in small groups in many parts of Britain, the
Commonwealth, Europe and America. There is also
a strong missionary interest in many of their assemblies.

EVENTS IN SCOTLAND

Early in the nineteenth century the evangelical party
in the Church of Scotland began to show marked
vitality under the brilliant leadership of Dr. Andrew
Thomson and Dr. Thomas Chalmers, men of deep
spiritual experience and great scholarship. In 1712 the
government had passed the Patronage Act which in-
fringed the right of the Scottish people to elect their
own ministers. It was a sore question and productive of
much evil.[1] In 1834, under the leadership of Dr.

[1] See p. 170.

Chalmers, the General Assembly passed the Veto Act giving congregations the right to reject the patron's nominee if they considered him unsuitable. When, however, the churches implemented this decision, their rights were flagrantly interfered with by the civil courts. Presbyteries were heavily fined, and ordered by the Court of Session to induct to the ministry unacceptable presentees of the patron even though they were opposed by nearly all the Church members and were utterly unfitted for the post.

The government was very badly served by its advisers and the House of Commons threw out the Petition presented to it by the Church by 211 votes to 76. Sir Robert Peel expressed the attitude of the government: 'I think it of the greatest importance that the spiritual authority of the Church should be restrained, as it is restrained, and made subordinate to Parliament.' He forgot that the Statutes of Scotland guaranteed the spiritual freedom of the Church. Even the General Assembly was threatened with interdicts in the discharge of its spiritual functions. In loyalty to 'the Crown Rights of the Redeemer', no less than 478 ministers left the Church of Scotland on May 18, 1843, carrying with them the old Confession of Faith and constitution of the Church of Scotland, and formed the Free Church of Scotland. Their action profoundly moved the nation and they were admired throughout Christendom. They gave up the privileges of their State connection and cast themselves on God. They lost their homes and endowments but kept the faith.

THE OXFORD MOVEMENT

The repeal of the obnoxious Test and Corporation Acts in 1828 and the permission to Roman Catholics and Nonconformists to sit in Parliament alarmed some of the Tory Churchmen at Oxford. They were appalled at the prospect of non-Anglicans voting on questions affecting the Church. A loud cry went up that the Church was in danger. John Henry Newman, then vicar of St. Mary's, Oxford, took up the challenge on behalf of the Established Church, ably assisted by Richard Hurrell Froude, Edward B. Pusey, Hugh James Rose (of Cambridge), and W. G. Ward. They put themselves forward as stalwart defenders of the Church of England and, in order to strengthen its position, they sought to prove its unbroken continuity with the ancient Catholic Church, and claimed that the Anglicans were the truest representatives of the Church of the Middle Ages. They believed that their Church was a middle way between Roman Catholicism and Protestantism. They extolled the power and prestige of the bishops and urged that their authority had descended to them by divine appointment from the apostles of Christ. They propagated their views by means of the publication of theses which they called *Tracts for the Times*. Thus they were known as 'Tractarians', but are frequently referred to as 'The Oxford Movement'. They glorified the past and stressed the place of tradition in the Church.

The leaders of the movement exerted a considerable influence. Sir Walter Scott's colourful descriptions of life in the Middle Ages had fostered an attitude in the country favourable to their outlook. John Keble, author of *The Christian Year*, had greatly influenced the Tractarian leaders in the earlier stages. Very soon their work culminated in a revival of Roman Catholic ideas and practices which had been thrown out of the Anglican Church at the Reformation. The most important plank in their scheme was the doctrine of apostolic succession. Through the laying on of hands, a special grace and authority was supposed to have descended to the bishops from the apostles. As usually conceived, the doctrine is mechanical, and has against it the fact that, in the course of the ages, many Church dignitaries, supposed to receive and transmit this grace and authority, were themselves obviously devoid of the grace of God. According to Newman, 'we must necessarily consider none to be really ordained' unless ordained by those in the apostolic succession. This unchurches a vast number of devoted Christian ministers.

In one of the Tracts, Newman claimed that clergymen were 'entrusted with the awful and mysterious gifts of making the bread and wine, Christ's Body and Blood'. As this doctrine of Transubstantiation was not officially promulgated in the Roman Church until the Lateran Council of 1215, and was unknown in the Early Church, one marvels how the Tractarians could regard such teaching as primitive and apostolic. In 1835, Dr. Pusey caused a sensation by publishing a Tract on Baptismal Regeneration which shocked not only the Evangelicals but even High Churchmen like Bishop Davenant. The leaders of the Oxford Movement professed loyalty to the constitution of the Church of England, but were clearly drifting Romewards. Thus Oakeley, an enthusiastic follower of Newman, wrote in *The British Critic* (the mouthpiece of the Movement) with regard to the Roman Church, 'we are estranged from her in presence, not in heart; may we never be provoked to forget her.' W. G. Ward, another eager disciple of Newman, wrote in 1842 of English Protestantism as a 'debased, hollow, inconsistent form of Christianity'.

The spirit and aims of the Oxford Movement are best shown in Tract XC issued by Newman in 1839. Although the formulation of the Thirty-Nine Articles was a definite indication that England was a Protestant country, Newman in this Tract tried to show that a man might sign these Articles and yet 'aim at being Catholic in heart and doctrine'. If, however, the Thirty-Nine Articles could be interpreted as Newman and his friends interpreted them, they were of no value whatever as a criterion of the faith of the Church of England. The University of Oxford and the bishops were speedily roused to action. The Hebdomadal Council condemned Tract XC outright and charged Newman with 'evasion' for thus trying to explain away the creed of the Anglican Church. The Bishop of Oxford (who had been friendly to Newman) declared: 'I cannot reconcile myself to a system of interpretation which is so subtle that by it the Articles may be made to mean anything or nothing.' Bishop after bishop followed in the same strain. Some were very frank and outspoken.

The Tractarians were freely accused by the public of being 'Jesuitical' and with practising 'evasion'. Their doctrine of 'reserve' and lack of frankness lent colour to the charge. In October 1845, Newman was formally received into the Roman Church, where he became a cardinal. Ward, Faber, Manning and other Tractarians followed the same path. Throughout the years many Anglo-Catholics have done likewise.

The changes wrought in a large section of the Anglican Church by the Oxford Movement have, however, been incredibly great. Bishop E. A. Knox wrote in 1933: 'Probably even Newman or Pusey would be astounded, if they could visit the scenes of their old labours, and could see bishops mitred and vested in copes and chasubles, clergy and churches so ornamented as to be indistinguishable from those of Rome, images of the Virgin with lights burning before them, pyxes, monstrances, and like evidences of worship of the Host, and could hear the Mass offered in Anglican Churches for the living and the dead.'[1]

The merit of the Reformation was that it went right back to Christ and the apostles for its teaching. The tragedy of the Oxford Movement is that its members turned their backs upon the Reformation and the principles for which Cranmer, Latimer, Ridley, and

[1] Bishop E. A. Knox, *The Tractarian Movement*, p. 360.

Hooper, great bishops of their own Church, had died at the stake. Instead they returned to the erroneous ideas of the Middle Ages.

ROMAN CATHOLICISM IN THE NINETEENTH CENTURY

In France the military genius and force of character of Napoleon soon raised him to the highest pinnacle of power. Since the French Revolution, the Roman Church had passed through many bitter experiences. Many thousands of the priests had been driven from the country, and many were put to death. Religious freedom was restored in 1795, but the pope refused to recognize the French Civil Constitution of the Clergy and, thereupon, in 1796 Napoleon marched on Rome and drove him into a humiliating acceptance of French demands.[1]

Soon the Gallican Articles of 1682 were restored and the pontiff was forbidden to interfere in the affairs of the French Church without governmental sanction. This led to much discontent among the clergy, who looked more and more to the pope across the Alps, and were therefore called 'Ultramontanists'. Protestants were given full religious freedom and their ministers were paid by the State.

In 1806, Francis II renounced the title of Emperor of the Holy Roman Empire which was first given to Charlemagne in 800. In spite of eagerness on the part of Pope Pius VII to placate Napoleon, a French army entered Rome in 1808, annexed the papal territories, and took the pope prisoner. The latter, however, returned in triumph to Rome in 1814 when Napoleon abdicated. With the final defeat of the Emperor of the French at Waterloo in 1815 there began a new era of prosperity for the papacy. The ungodliness of the Revolutionary period had produced a strong reaction against atheism and in favour of the Roman Church.

[1] See also p. 171.

The Jesuits had been busy propagandists in this period alleging that all the evils which had overtaken the nations were due to the worship of reason, disloyalty to the Catholic faith, and in particular the suppression of the Jesuit Order. On August 7, 1814, Pope Pius VII revived the Order which Pope Clement XIV had suppressed in 1773.

The Jesuits were welcomed back with open arms and not only regained their position of power in Roman Catholic countries, but found a footing in Protestant lands such as Holland, England and the United States. They exercised a great influence through their tremendous grip on schools and colleges, and implanted a hard intolerance in many minds.

For centuries the Roman Church had claimed to be infallible, and there had been much debate as to where this infallibility lay. The Jesuits insisted, for their own ends, that infallibility rested in the pope alone. They persuaded Pope Pius IX in 1854 to promulgate, without consulting his Council, the doctrine of the Immaculate Conception of the Virgin Mary—that she was born without original sin. In taking this line, the pontiff had practically claimed infallible authority. The next step was taken at the Vatican Council of 1869-70 where, again through Jesuit influence, the doctrine of Papal Infallibility was decreed on July 18, 1870. This teaches that when the Roman pontiff, speaking 'ex cathedra', defines a doctrine regarding faith or morals, 'he is infallible, by virtue of his supreme apostolic authority.' In the Council there was a great weight of learning against the proposal. Nevertheless the arguments of those in favour of the declaration of infallibility easily prevailed. From then on, the Jesuits had more power than ever at the Vatican.

Because of the immense number of immigrants which entered the United States in the nineteenth century from the Roman Catholic areas of Europe and from Ireland, the Roman Church became very powerful there. As the nation developed and became prosperous, so did the Church of Rome. In Britain also there was a marked increase in the numbers and strength of this Church, and the century witnessed the removal of the political disabilities under which its members formerly laboured. In Latin America, where Protestants were very few, the Catholic Church grew in strength as the various States developed politically, economically, and numerically. Liberalism was, however, very strong in Latin American Universities and in most Latin American lands there developed eventually a strong anti-clerical undercurrent, especially among the educated classes.

NINETEENTH CENTURY REVIVALS

As one looks at the Protestant Churches in Britain and America, in the second part of the nineteenth century, the impression given is one of abounding vitality. It was an age when rationalism and scepticism were spreading in many sectors of the population. Nevertheless, for the mass of the people, loyalty to the gospel call and to the Church was a notable feature of the time. It was an era of great theologians and great preachers, and the churches were excellently attended. It is questionable whether the power of the pulpit on such a wide scale was ever so marked in the English-speaking world as it was in the years from 1840 to 1890. There were, indeed, giants in those days and we have only to think of some of the great names of the period to realize how mighty was their appeal. It has never been adequately realized, however, how much this period owed to the great revival movements which took place. This is particularly true of the 1857-60 revival. As a result of this work of the Holy Spirit, at least one million converts were received into the Church of God in the United States alone—a large proportion of the population in those days. From America it spread first to Ulster and then to England and Scotland. In Britain, as in America, it was seen to be a work of God, not of man; and in this country, also, a million new members were added to the churches.

The tremendous effect of this can scarcely be exaggerated.[1] It came to many congregations as life from the dead. One of the great results was the effect produced upon William Booth and his wife which led to the founding in 1865 of the Salvation Army which has brought so much blessing to many far-separated countries of the world. This organization was strongly opposed at first but is now recognized in most countries as a mighty force in evangelistic and philanthropic work.

Again it was through the influence of the revival that Thomas Barnardo was converted in 1862. The story of the establishing of his orphan homes is typical of the great upsurge of philanthropic activity during this period which derived its vitality and earnestness from the evangelical convictions of those who shared in it. Much of this activity was directed towards helping children and, as the century progressed, many Societies were founded which had as their objective the promotion of the physical and spiritual welfare of boys and girls. Earlier, in 1844, George Williams, a young draper's assistant, had founded the Young Men's Christian Association. Its branches helped on the revival and in their turn were greatly stimulated by it. In 1859, for example, a Conference of provincial and London delegates resolved to emphasize anew one of their early principles that all members of branches should have experienced 'a decided and well-authenticated conversion to God'. This was the spirit underlying many of the great movements of the century.

Looking back we might say that one of the most notable events of the revival movement in North America was the conversion of Dwight L. Moody at

[1] See Edwin Orr, *The Second Evangelical Awakening*, Chapter XV.

Chicago in 1857, when he was twenty years old. He entered upon a business career in the Middle West but later felt called to become an evangelist. He began his great work among the wildest and most ungodly young men of Chicago. In 1870 he was joined by Ira D. Sankey whose power as a singer profoundly touched men's hearts. In 1873 the two men came to Britain and held meetings in most of the large cities, and even in some small towns, with astonishing results. There was no sensationalism about Moody's presentation of the gospel. Its most remarkable feature was the way in which it affected men and women of all classes, educated and illiterate, rich and poor. The evangelists made several visits to Britain at intervals of some years and always with the same results. Vast numbers professed conversion. In America also their influence became immense.

As a result of the spiritual quickening of this period there arose the Keswick Movement, closely associated with the work of D. L. Moody but scarcely the result of it. In 1874, and again in 1875, a number of evangelical leaders, who had been influenced by the writings of three Americans, T. C. Upham, Asa Mahan and W. E. Boardman, on the importance of the Spirit-filled life, arranged Conventions at which special teaching on this subject was given. Among those who were greatly influenced by these early gatherings were the Rev. T. D. Harford-Battersby, vicar of Keswick, Cumberland, and a Mr. Robert Wilson, a Quaker, who lived at Workington in the same county. They resolved to call a Convention at Keswick and the first small gathering was held in 1875. Since then the Convention has met every year in the same place, except for the period of the two world wars, and its influence has become worldwide. Thousands gather every year in the small lakeside town, and similar Conventions have come into being, often with the name 'Keswick', in all parts of the world.

WITNESS IN THE UNIVERSITIES

We referred in an earlier chapter to the outstanding work of Charles Simeon in Cambridge at the end of the eighteenth and the beginning of the nineteenth centuries.[1] He revived an evangelical tradition within the university and his influence lived on long after his death in 1836. Forty years later, in November 1876, the Cambridge Inter-Collegiate Christian Union was formed, the first of many similar student groups which have since sprung up in all the British universities and in many other places of higher education as well. Three years later a similar Christian Union was founded at Oxford.

The formation of these groups should be seen against the wider background of spiritual interest aroused in all the universities as a result of the revival taking place in the country as a whole. In quite a number of colleges and medical schools, prayer groups were meeting regularly. In 1882, D. L. Moody was invited by the C.I.C.C.U. to conduct a mission in Cambridge. In spite of considerable prejudice, and a certain amount of initial rowdyism, the mission was a great success and many undergraduates were converted. Two years later 'The Cambridge Seven', a group of gifted men, the majority of them well-known in society or in sport, astonished the student world by volunteering to go out as missionaries to China. Before sailing some of them visited other universities, addressing crowded gathering of students and arousing a great deal of interest.[2]

Just at this time, Robert Wilder, a student at Princeton, formed a small society to pray that God would provide a thousand volunteers for the mission field. By 1886 American students had been themselves pro-

---

[1] See p. 169.
[2] The full story can be read in *The Cambridge Seven*, by J. C. Pollock I.V.F., 3s. 6d.

foundly moved by accounts reaching them from Britain of the evangelical movement within the univerversities and especially by the action of the Cambridge Seven. That year at Mount Hermon School, Massachusetts, in a meeting presided over by D. L. Moody, a hundred students volunteered for missionary service and the Student Volunteer Movement was launched, with Wilder as its moving spirit. He and J. N. Forman made several visits to the British Isles and aroused immense enthusiasm with the rallying cry 'The Evangelization of the World in this generation'. The movement was officially inaugurated in Britain at a conference in Edinburgh, in 1892. The aim was to inspire students to volunteer for the mission field. Over nine thousand did so in the first quarter of a century following its launching in America. It became necessary to lay stress on the spiritual life of students in the colleges and universities at home, and this led to the founding of many Christian Unions. In 1905 the movement linking these groups became known as the Student Christian Movement (S.C.M.). It was closely allied from the start with the World Student Christian Federation which had been formed ten years earlier.

From 1890 onwards, John R. Mott was the greatest figure in the Volunteer Movement. He had set out to study law at Cornell University, but through an interview with Kynaston Studd, brother of C. T. Studd of the Cambridge Seven and a President of the C.I.C.C.U., his whole life was changed. He became a fervent evangelist and the recognized leader of the Student Movement. He was a man of remarkable personality and a born organizer. Under him the Student Movement became a mighty force throughout the world.

By the end of the nineteenth century, and more particularly in the earlier part of the twentieth century, it became apparent that the S.C.M. had lost much of its early evangelical fervour. Its leaders by 1907 had come to regard the 'Bible Christian' outlook of men like Moody and Wilder, as somewhat naïve. The need for personal salvation was little stressed and the place of the 'social gospel' was more and more emphasized The daring speculations of the liberal critics of the Bible and the unwise and sweeping conclusions of students of Comparative Religion were received with remarkable credulity. Indeed, many questioned even the statements of the historic Catholic creeds with regard to our Lord. The result was a serious weakening of the Christian testimony so nobly borne previously within the universities and schools.

The fact that in March 1910 the C.I.C.C.U. felt compelled, from conscientious motives, to disaffiliate from the Student Christian Movement reveals how far-reaching the changes in the S.C.M. had been. The C.I.C.C.U. still wished to maintain its historical position. Writing of their evangelical principles J. C. Pollock describes them thus: 'They accepted humbly the authority and inspiration of the Bible. Secondly, they believed firmly that God had acted in Christ to save men. The Cross of Christ was at the very centre of their theology . . . acknowledging Christ's death as nothing less than substitutionary, and accepting it as the only ground of man's forgiveness. . . . They were convinced that without the new birth no true life was possible.'[1]

MATERIALISM AND UNBELIEF

In the English-speaking world the remarkable evangelical revivals of the nineteenth century brought results which were immeasurably great, not only from a religious but from a social point of view. They affected all sections of the people and helped to save the labouring classes from the atheism which began openly to manifest itself in other lands. At the same time, however, mighty movements of a hostile character were growing up parallel with those we have described,

[1] *A Cambridge Movement*, p. 44.

and we must now trace the growth of these, especially on the Continent of Europe.

In many countries rationalism kept manifesting itself during much of the century, causing division and weakness among the churches. Men like Strauss (1808-1874), and Baur (1792-1860), explained away the miracles and other supernatural elements in the Bible, and regarded Christianity as a natural development of human ideas without any divine intervention. The writings of Charles Darwin on the *Origin of Species by Natural Selection*, of John Stuart Mill, propounding semi-sceptical ideas, and of Herbert Spencer on agnosticism, did much to unsettle faith.

The unexampled prosperity of the second half of the century, and the eager desire to amass wealth quickly, tended to foster a materialistic outlook. Thus, spiritual interests were relegated by many to a secondary place, and the pursuit of pleasure loomed ever more largely in the public eye. The new theories in science were often misunderstood by the man in the street and the idea grew up that there was an irreconcilable conflict between religion and science. There was a widespread failure to realize that it was only certain schools of philosophy that were at war with religion, and that the true facts of science (as distinct from unproved theories) were not antagonistic to the Bible when rightly interpreted. There was much misunderstanding on both sides and much controversy, and the faith of a considerable number was shaken.

It was, however, the application of a rationalistic criticism to the Bible which proved most serious for the Church. Since the days of Astruc and Eichhorn in the eighteenth century, Biblical scholars, especially on the Continent, had been occupied with the new critical methods; but the average minister had taken little notice of their work. By the fourth quarter of the nineteenth century, however, the rank and file of the ministry were profoundly unsettled by the new outlook and even the man in the pew was often disturbed.

According to the Graf-Wellhausen view, which came to be generally accepted, the traditionally received beliefs regarding the Bible were turned upside down. The writings of the prophets were placed first in chronological order and the Books of the Law, formerly ascribed to Moses (1300 or 1400 B.C.), were now regarded as mostly written in the period of Ezra after his return from the Exile in 458 B.C. The greater part of the Psalms was also placed in the post-exilic period. There have always been some differences of opinion among liberal scholars, but it may be said that, in the main, their more radical representatives at this time were very chary about believing in miracles, and tried their best to reduce the supernatural element in the Bible to a minimum. This was particularly so with regard to the predictive element in prophecy. On this account they sought to give writings a late date to show that the prophets were dealing with history, not with prediction. It is somewhat awkward for them, however, that the prophets themselves constantly claimed to be fore-telling the future. The more advanced 'higher critics' had, naturally, a new conception of the divine inspiration of the Scriptures. It was very different from the view, previously accepted by all branches of the historic Christian Church, that 'all scripture is given by inspiration of God' (2 Tim. iii. 16), and is reliable because it is the work of 'holy men of God' who were 'moved by the Holy Ghost' (2 Pet. i. 21). The claim was regularly made that the new critical method was scientific. On this account the idea became common that a pronouncement by a leading member of the critical school must be as reliable as a deduction in mathematics, or as some discovery in the physical sciences made through the inductive method. The fact is that, as often as not, the confident declarations of destructive critics were based merely on subjective considerations and could not by any stretch of imagination be regarded as scientific. Views were often put forward without a shred of evidence. Because he was regarded as an authority, a leading critic could find unquestioning acceptance for the most extravagant statements.

There was much opposition to the new views. Bishop Colenso in Natal was excommunicated by his ecclesiastical superior when he declared in 1862 that the historical existence of Moses was doubtful and that Joshua was certainly mythical. In 1881, Professor W. Robertson Smith was removed by the Free Church of Scotland from the Chair of Hebrew at Aberdeen because of his critical views. In many quarters there was consternation at the teachings of the new school; but long before the end of the century their point of view was accepted on a widespread scale in most of the churches. This was a revolution of the first magnitude, the vast consequences of which are not yet fully realized by the average member of the Church. Among the scholarly pioneers of the new movement were Stanley, Cheyne, and Driver in England; A. B. Davidson, Robertson Smith, and G. A. Smith in Scotland; and Briggs, Harper and Toy in America.

The same method was applied to the critical study of the New Testament, and there has since been a good deal of confusion in this very important field. The confusion was increased by the rise of Form Criticism in Germany in 1919 under the leadership of Dibelius, Bultmann, and Schmidt, who claimed that by this method they could construct the original gospel stories which, they alleged, are reported erroneously in the New Testament. As a result of these 'reconstructions' many Christians have been unsettled in their beliefs. The powerful rationalistic and critical influences which in the last hundred years have proved so serious a menace to the faith of the Churches emanated from Germany more than from any other country.

For a long time Britain was saved from feeling these

influences to any marked degree among the lay members of the Churches because of the great movements of evangelical revival which had repeatedly visited the land as already recorded. It was only in the twentieth century, when the force of these movements had died down, that the devastating effects of liberalism began to be fully apparent.

During the nineteenth century all the leading Churches historically associated with Britain found a place in the United States and grew and flourished with the phenomenal development of the country. As a result of the flood of immigrants from Europe, the Lutherans and the Dutch Reformed Churches became strongly represented. Many Jews also entered the country. Swedenborgians, Mormons, the Church of God, the Unitarians, Seventh Day Adventists and many other deviationist groups became more prominent, and some of these have become large bodies in the course of the years. There is nothing more remarkable in history than the development of the United States, socially, economically and religiously in the last century and a half. It has stood for religious freedom with equal rights for all, with most beneficial results. When we remember that in 1860 the United States had only thirty million inhabitants, and that today it has well over 160 million, we realize what a colossal task the Churches have faced in providing religious ordinances for the people as they spread ever onwards towards new frontiers. The vitality and foresight of Church and people enabled them not only to discharge this mighty task at home but to share with Britain in pouring forth a stream of men and money for the evangelization of the world.

CHAPTER XXII

THE TWENTIETH CENTURY

BEFORE THE FIRST WORLD WAR

NOTHING could exceed the confidence with which the Protestant Church entered upon the twentieth century. Under the impulse of Darwin's theory of evolution it was believed that progress was inevitable. The world was getting better and better and the Church was pictured as going on from one triumph to another. Mankind had left behind well-nigh all the dark traces of the 'ape and tiger' and was entering upon a new era of high spiritual idealism and universal peace. It was the heyday of liberalism. Biblical critics boasted of their 'assured results', the majority of them unfavourable to what had always been the orthodox view of Scripture. For a long time it had been the fashion to send all aspiring theological students to finish their studies in German Universities. It was from these centres that the most radical theories of Biblical criticism emanated, and it was not long before these views were being vigorously propagated elsewhere.

The civilized world had become rich beyond anything that former ages could have dreamt of. The figure of the multi-millionaire fascinated men, especially in Britain and America. Few seem to have stopped to think that these bright prospects might not endure. The feeling rather was that 'tomorrow shall be as this day and much more abundant'. The working classes were looking forward hopefully to the future because of their ever-growing political power. The capitalists and the aristocracy were still entrenched in positions of privilege and quite unconscious that in a few short years the ground would be shaking under their feet. A few discerning people feared that what was true of Ephraim of old was then true of our modern civilization: 'Strangers have devoured his strength, and he knoweth it not.'[1]

In religious matters scepticism was increasing. Robert Blatchford and *The Clarion* championed agnosticism and had many followers in the English cities. Church attendances were not quite so good as in the previous generation. Preachers generally did not now seem to preach with the same note of authority and power as their predecessors. Love of pleasure was taking an increasing hold upon the people. The Lord's Day was becoming increasingly a day for amusement and less a day of rest and worship. The evils of drink, gambling, and immorality continued to provide cause for uneasiness. In spite of such matters, however, the man-in-the-street remained well satisfied and assured. In the Church, in spite of the increasing number of ministers who preached the 'New Theology', and in spite of the growing materialism of their hearers, a large section of the people continued to be influenced by the great spiritual tradition inherited from former days. But in general it may be said that congregations lacked the fire which comes from a personal baptism of the Holy Spirit.

Then came the stunning blow of August 1914, when the First World War began. Long cherished ideas as to the inevitability of progress, the superiority of German culture, and the high spiritual attainments of the twentieth-century world, were rudely shattered. That brilliant statesman-philosopher, A. J. Balfour, declared that, like many, he had made the mistake of thinking that, because the world had progressed materially and scientifically, it must have made equal progress morally and spiritually. It was a rude awakening. As the terrible

[1] Hosea vii. 9.

toll of war piled up, and atrocities and barbarities succeeded one another, and 'man's inhumanity to man' became ever more apparent, it was driven in on many that the Bible's account of man's lost, sinful and depraved condition, apart from the grace of God, was true after all, and that men could be saved only through faith in Christ alone.

When, after four-and-a-half years of blood and terror and the loss of ten million young lives, peace came to a battered world, the theologians and the Biblical critics in the churches were in a more chastened mood than for many years. Liberalism in theology which had held pride of a place for a generation began to take a humbler station. Many hard things were said about it, even by some who had been its friends.

NEO-ORTHODOXY

By no one was the liberal school more scathingly condemned than by Karl Barth, a young Swiss minister. He immediately leapt into fame. He appealed constantly to the Bible and the Reformers, and his theology claimed to be a 'theology of the Word'. He used terms which had long been laid aside, such as 'the fall', 'original sin', 'atonement', and 'justification'. He even referred to 'verbal inspiration'. At first many conservative theologians were delighted. They felt that here was the man to lead the world back to the Bible and to the doctrines of the Reformers. They were doomed to disappointment. Not only was his dialectic very difficult to understand, but he seemed to change his position frequently. Worse than this he gave expression in his *Dogmatik* to sentiments such as these: The Bible is 'all the way through fallible human words' (Vol. 1, p. 565); the prophets and the apostles are fallible men even when writing God's revelation (p. 558); and the liability of the Bible to mistakes 'also covers its *religious,* that is its theological contents' (p. 565). In his *Commentary on Romans,* Barth declared that the teachings of Jesus as given in the

Gospels are far from the truth about God. It is thus apparent that Barth accepts many of the findings of the most radical and destructive critics of the Bible. Nevertheless, he believes that the Spirit of God, when He has an 'encounter' with a man, takes this very fallible and contradictory book and uses it for his conversion. It then *becomes* the Word of God to him. Hence the Church must preach the Bible, for the great work of the Church is to bring it to men.

This theological system, originated over thirty years ago by Barth and Brunner and now known as Neo-Orthodoxy or Neo-Calvinism, has found acceptance in a wide circle in Europe, the British Commonwealth, and America. It appeals to those who are alive to the dangers of the older liberalism, but who cannot bring themselves to accept the orthodox views of Scripture and Christian doctrine.

ROMAN CATHOLIC GAINS AND LOSSES

Throughout the world generally there has been a marked display of activity on the part of the Roman Church since early in the nineteenth century. This is shown in missionary activities, in the establishment of new religious Orders, in the reintroduction of old Orders into places where they had fallen into abeyance and in the generous financial support given by Catholics to their Church. With the growth of the democratic spirit, the Roman Church has been careful to appeal to the labouring classes and has known what would impress the popular mind. Hence the widespread erection of splendid buildings, the organization of large colourful processions and the cultivation of gorgeous ceremonial. Especially in Britain and America full advantage has been taken of the splendid educational facilities provided by the State. Nevertheless, the Roman Church has suffered much from her own children. Witness the remarkable growth of Communism in lands like Italy and France, with its menacing attitude to the Church, the definite hostility of hundreds of thousands of Spaniards in the days of the Republic in the recent past, the changed circumstances in Poland and Hungary with the appearance of Soviet government, and the demonstrations against the Church in Argentine in 1955 by the followers of President Perón.

Since the last quarter of the nineteenth century Protestant missions in Latin America have gained greatly in strength and the Protestants in these nations now number several millions. Where formerly it was prohibited to open a non-Catholic place of worship, and where it was forbidden to bury Protestants in the cemeteries, very considerable progress has been made in the direction of greater liberty. Latin American countries since the days of the Spanish Conquest had denied religious freedom to all who were not Roman Catholics. Under the impact of liberal ideas in the nineteenth century, however, one country after another revised its constitution and granted religious toleration to all creeds. The last to do this was Peru in 1915. But usually these countries draw a sharp distinction between *religious toleration* and *religious freedom*, and their conception of toleration is generally more limited than in English-speaking lands. The result is that under certain circumstances non-Catholics can still be subject to serious disabilities as, for example, in Colombia at the present time where many Protestants have been killed and their places of worship destroyed. Generally speaking, however, there is now in Latin American countries a gratifying recognition of religious freedom.

In October 1950, the Roman Church promulgated the dogma of the Assumption of Mary, declaring that the body of the Virgin had ascended miraculously to heaven soon after her death. The matter had been debated for centuries and it is remarkable that it is only in this enlightened age that every Catholic should be obliged to exercise such credulity as to believe this doctrine. The same reflection applies to the dogma of Papal Infallibility[1] which had never been promulgated officially until the scientific, progressive days of the nineteenth century, but which must now be accepted by every Roman Catholic.

BIBLICAL CHRISTIANITY

Since the end of the Second World War the conservative evangelical school of thought in Great Britain and America has been stronger and more vigorous than for many years. In the theological world there has been a new and welcome interest in conservative scholarship, and a literature is being built up in which conservative views are ably stated and vigorously defended. In the churches there has been a renewed emphasis upon evangelism arising out of, and in some cases closely modelled upon, the large-scale evangelistic campaigns arranged for Dr. Billy Graham. This revival of evangelicalism and the large numbers of men holding conservative views, who are offering for the ministry, seems to be causing church leaders in many denominations some quite considerable concern. This is seen in the repeated attacks on 'fundamentalism', and the endeavour to build up a picture of all conservatives as obscurantist in their thinking.

In Britain many of these attacks have been centred on The Inter-Varsity Fellowship of Evangelical Unions. This Society was brought into existence in 1928. Nine years previously an Annual Inter-Varsity Conference of Evangelical Unions had been organized by Oxford and Cambridge undergraduates who desired to see Christian Unions similar to the C.I.C.C.U.[2] in all the universities. During the inter-war years many such groups were founded and were affiliated to the Inter-Varsity Fellowship. The I.V.F., with its strong conservative doctrinal basis, has greatly expanded its work during the last

[1] See p. 191.   [2] See p. 195.

fifteen years, and affiliated organizations are now at work in the Training and Technical Colleges. The movement also spread to Canada, Australia, and New Zealand, and from Canada later entered the United States. Independent National Fellowships were formed, all of them basing their activity, as did the old Student Volunteer Movement, on a deep conviction that the Bible is the 'Word of God' and on a desire to stimulate personal faith and to further evangelical work.

THE CHURCHES' INFLUENCE ON THE PEOPLE

It will be seen that the general situation in the Protestant Churches today leaves much to be desired. Theologically there is chaos; it is a commonplace to find men in the same denomination holding views which are as wide apart as the poles. This is one result of the revolt against dogma which became so widespread in theological circles in the last quarter of the nineteenth century when the fashionable cry was that doctrine did not matter. This led to the relaxation of creed subscription in most of the large denominations. Declarations were skilfully framed to allow men to interpret the Confession of Faith or Articles of their particular Church in a variety of ways. The net result was that these confessional statements came to mean little, except as a historical record of what was once the Creed of the Church. Some of the smaller religious bodies and one or two larger ones have refused to compromise and are standing on the old foundations; but apart from them the changes in theological outlook have been revolutionary. The benefits expected from this so-called 'progressive' policy have not materialized. Instead, it is widely recognized now that the Churches are facing a crisis. Except in North America, where statistics show that sixty per cent. of the whole population regularly attend church, there is a very marked decrease in church going. Not infrequently the Church has come to look to secular attractions to bolster up its dwindling influence.

Thus in the halls of some churches one finds dances. whist drives and all kinds of secular activities in abundance, while the once honoured Prayer-Meeting and Bible Study groups are notably absent. In too many pulpits the great doctrines of the faith have been forgotten and only the social gospel is preached. Dr. H. R. Niebuhr speaks of modern preaching as presenting 'a God without wrath who brought men without sin into a kingdom without judgment, through the ministrations of a Christ without a cross'.[1]

In an address to the Classical Association at Oxford, about two years ago, that outstanding scholar, Professor Gilbert Murray, made the ominous declaration that all over Europe, from West to East, civilization was disintegrating, and gave solid reasons for his statement. Equally ominous was the statement of such a keen observer as Dr. Garbett, a former Archbishop of York, made early in 1954, that the lack of religion in Great Britain was now 'beginning to produce a visible moral degeneracy'. Other Christian leaders on both sides of the Atlantic have expressed themselves in similar terms.

THE ECUMENICAL MOVEMENT

In nothing is the ecclesiastical history of the twentieth century more remarkable than in the growing tendency to unity among the Protestant Churches. We can do no more than mention some of the trends:

1. The formation of the Free Church Council in England in 1892, and the Federal Council of Evangelical Churches in 1919. 2. The union of the majority of the Free Church of Scotland with the United Presbyterian Church to form the United Free Church of Scotland in 1900, while the conservative minority continued as the Free Church of Scotland under the old constitution. 3. The union of a majority of the Presbyterian Church of Canada with the Congregational and Methodist Churches of Canada in 1925 to form the

[1] H. R. Niebuhr, *The Kingdom of God in America*, pp. 192 f.

United Church of Canada—now the largest Protestant denomination in the country. The minority in the Presbyterian Church continued under the old name. 4. The union of the Church of Scotland with the majority of the United Free Church in 1929, which brought an overwhelming majority of the people of Scotland into the National Church. Again, a minority carried on as the United Free Church. 5. The union of almost all the various Methodist bodies in England in 1932 to form one large United Church. 6. The formation of the Church of South India in 1947 through the union of the Anglican, Congregational and Presbyterian Churches, under an Episcopal polity. 7. The entrance of the Anglican Church into inter-communion with the Lutheran Church of Sweden, and several Synods of the Eastern Orthodox Church. 8. The formation of the Federal Council of Christian Churches in the United States.

Ever since the Oxford Movement, the Anglo-Catholics have showed themselves anxious for a closer under standing with the Church of Rome. In 1896, however, the pope pronounced emphatically against the recognition of Anglican Orders. When theologians of the English Church and the Roman Church carried on discussions at Malines from 1921 onwards under the aegis of Cardinal Mercier, the pope ended them by declaring that no union would be acceptable unless based on complete submission to the Roman See. In view of the powerful influence of the Anglo-Catholics and the tendencies revealed in these conversations, the decisive rejection of the Revised Prayer Book of the Anglican Church in 1928 by the British House of Commons, brought great relief to many Protestants, for it was an indication that loyalty to Reformation ideals was still a vital force in England.

For over thirty years no subject has been so much discussed in Church circles as reunion. The modern ecumenical movement dates from the momentous Edinburgh Missionary Conference of 1910. Out of it arose the Conferences on Faith and Order at Lausanne, in 1927, and Edinburgh, in 1937, and the Conferences on Life and Work, the first of which was held at Stockholm in 1925. These lines of approach were united in the World Council of Churches which was founded at Amsterdam in 1948. The great international Missionary Conferences at Jerusalem in 1928, and Tambaram, India, in 1938, pointed the way for such a consummation. At the first meeting of the World Council, delegates were present from 147 churches and 44 different countries. Several overtures have been made to the Roman Church but they have consistently refused to join.

Various sections of Protestant Christians have had misgivings about the principles and aims of the World Council. The opposition has found vocal expression in the National Association of Evangelicals (U.S.A.); the International Council of Christian Churches; the Reformed Ecumenical Synod; and the British Evangelical Council. The opposition is based on fear of liberalism on the one hand, and of Catholicism, working through the Eastern Orthodox Church and the Anglo-Catholics, on the other. Without doubt, however, the World Council of Churches is a most powerful force in the ecclesiastical life of the twentieth century.

TAKING STOCK

As we look at the life of the Churches throughout the world today, what impresses us most is the rich fruit which has followed upon the labour and sacrifice of the missionary pioneers of the late eighteenth and early nineteenth century. They sowed the seed often in blood and tears, and other men have entered into their labours. We see in many countries how vigorous young Churches are taking their places confidently by the side of the older Churches of other lands. There are problems in plenty; closed doors in China and the lands behind the Iron Curtain; the growing difficulty of work in Islamic countries; the terrible problems caused by unwise handling of racial questions, as in South Africa; the rise of a fanatical nationalism in many parts of the world; and the serious impact of materialistic and Communistic forces upon peoples awaking, through education, from the sleep of ages.

In spite of all these problems, and others besides, there is very much to inspire confidence and thankfulness. In 1949 the total population of the world was estimated at 2,377 millions. Of these, 700 millions, or approximately $29\frac{1}{2}$ per cent. were Christians, at least nominally. In 1800 there were 960 millions in the world, of whom 174 millions (or about 19 per cent.) were reckoned as Christians. Looking at the percentages, we see that there has been progress, but not so much as to permit any slackening in the effort which is being made. Of the leading Christian bodies in the world, approximately thirty-one per cent. are Protestant, forty-eight per cent. Roman Catholic, and twenty-one per cent. Eastern Orthodox.

While the two World Wars have had an evil effect upon religious life in general, the interest in Missions has been wonderfully sustained to this hour, and there is scarcely any country where the gospel has not penetrated in greater or less degree. The future is not very clear, but we know that the Lord who went before His people in the pillar of cloud by day and the pillar of fire by night has not forgotten His believing Church in these modern days.

BIBLIOGRAPHY

I. GENERAL INTRODUCTION

Williston Walker. *A History of the Christian Church* (T. & T. Clark, 1949). This is good and easily obtained.

G. P. Fisher. *History of the Church* (Hodder & Stoughton, 1914). From apostolic times to 1887.

S. G. Green. *A Handbook of Church History* (R.T.S., 1904). From apostolic times to the Reformation.

E. L. Cutts. *Turning Points of General Church History* (S.P.C.K., 1928).

II. BOOKS ON SPECIAL PERIODS

Charles Hole. *A Manual of English Church History* (Church Book Room Press, 1910).

F. F. Bruce. *The Dawn of Christianity* (Paternoster Press, 1950). On the first and second centuries; and *The Growing Day* (A.D. 70 to 313) (Paternoster Press, 1951).

H. M. Gwatkin. *Early Church History to* A.D. *313*, 2 Vols. (Macmillan, 1927). An admirable work.

B. J. Kidd. *A History of the Church to* A.D. *451*, 3 Vols. (Oxford University Press, 1922). Detailed and very thorough.

G. Bartoli. *The Primitive Church and the Primacy of Rome* (Hodder & Stoughton, 1910).

Andre Lagarde. *Latin Church in the Middle Ages* (T. & T. Clark, 1915).

Margaret Deansley. *History of the Medieval Church, 590-1500* (Methuen, 1928).

Diana Leatham. *Celtic Sunrise* (Hodder & Stoughton, 1951). An excellent outline of Celtic Christianity.

J. A. Duke. *The Columban Church* (Oxford University Press, 1932).

Robert Rainy. *Ancient Catholic Church,* A.D. *98-451* (T. & T. Clark, 1902).

T. M. Lindsay. *History of the Reformation,* 2 Vols. (T. & T. Clark, 1906). The best work on the Reformation.

M. W. Patterson. *A History of the Church of England* (Longmans, 1925).

E. A. Payne. *The Free Church Tradition in the Life of England* (S.C.M. Press, 1944).

D. Hay Fleming. *The Reformation in Scotland* (Hodder & Stoughton, 1910). The work of a master.

Donald Maclean. *Aspects of Scottish Church History* (T. & T. Clark, 1927).

Alexander Smellie. *Men of the Covenant* (Andrew Melrose, 1924). The classic work on the Scottish Covenanters.

Henry Townsend. *The Claims of the English Free Churches* (Hodder & Stoughton, 1949).

A. R. MacEwan. *A History of the Church of Scotland,* 2 Vols. (Hodder & Stoughton, 1915). From A.D. 397 to 1560.

J. S. Simon. *The Revival of Religion in England in the Eighteenth Century* (Robert Culley).

J. Bready. *England Before and After Wesley* (Hodder & Stoughton, 1938).

A. F. Mitchell. *The Westminster Assembly* (Nisbet, 1883). A dispassionate discussion of the conflict between Puritans and Laudian Churchmen.

E. A. Knox. *The Tractarian Movement* (Putnam, 1933). Valuable in the study of Anglo-Catholic development.

Hensley Henson. *The Church of England* (Cambridge University Press, 1939).

J. Edwin Orr. *The Second Evangelical Awakening in*

Britain (Marshall, Morgan & Scott, 1949). Very valuable.

G. D. Henderson. *The Claims of the Church of Scotland* (Hodder & Stoughton, 1951).

G. N. M. Collins. *Whose Faith Follow* (Free Church of Scotland Publications). A brief history of the Disruption, and the Free Church of Scotland.

J. W. C. Wand. *History of the Modern Church from 1500 till 1929* (Methuen, 1929).

III. FOR EXTENSIVE READING

K. S. Latourette. *A History of the Expansion of Christianity*, 7 Vols. (Eyre & Spottiswoode, 1945). From apostolic times till 1914.

Philip Schaff. *History of the Christian Church*, 7 Vols. (Charles Scribner's Sons, New York, 1910). Earlier editions 1885 and 1888 by T. & T. Clark.

H. H. Milman. *History of Latin Christianity*, 9 Vols. (John Murray, 1872). A very readable work.

INDEX